BULLS

Da Champs!

NANCY STONE

BULLS

Da Champs!

by the
Chicago Tribune staff

TRIBUNE
PUBLISHING
Orlando, Florida
1992

EDITORS
Bruce Carden, Bob Condor

ART DIRECTOR/DESIGNER
Bill Henderson

PRODUCTION EDITOR
Ken Paskman

PICTURE EDITOR
Tim Broekema

TRIBUNE PUBLISHING
CONTRIBUTING EDITORS/WRITERS
Joy Dickinson, Bill Doughty, Dixie Kasper, Kathleen M. Kiely,
Gene Kruckemyer, Tim Povtak, David Wisor

TRIBUNE PUBLISHING
EDITORIAL RESEARCH
Ric Russo

For information about this and other
books from Tribune Publishing, contact:
TRIBUNE PUBLISHING
P.O. Box 1100
Orlando, Florida 32802-1100
(407) 420-5680

Library of Congress Catalog Card Number:
92-64373
ISBN 0-941263-57-6 (hard cover)
ISBN 0-941263-59-2 (soft cover)

Without you guys' support, no way would we have done it twice. Without you guys' support, there's no way we're going to be able to do it for the third time.

— **MICHAEL JORDAN**

CHARLES CHERNEY

CONTENTS

OPENING TIP   1
Taking their rightful place among the best ever, the Bulls found real satisfaction in a second title.

WARMUPS   4
The rings for the first championship arrived and so did the new challenges of chasing another title.

STARTING LINEUP   10
The crew varied widely, from superstar to journeyman, and each member gladly accepted his role.

FIRST HALF   26
The regular season is anything but regular when there is an NBA title to defend and another to seek.

HALFTIME   34
Tradition-rich Chicago Stadium soon will fade into the past, but its final few years are looking grand.

SECOND HALF   40
The playoffs started smoothly, then the Bulls met some tougher-than-expected resistance.

OVERTIME   60
There were a few slips in the NBA Finals against Portland, but some unlikely stars secured the title.

PARTY TIME!   76
This was coronation time for the Bulls, who shared a special moment of celebration with their fans.

THREE-PEAT?   84
The Bulls' repeat inspires a call for a three-peat as Michael Jordan starts looking ahead to next season.

OPENING TIP

The Bulls overcome all challenges to declare their dominance

When the Bulls strutted back onto the Chicago Stadium basketball court after winning the NBA title for a second straight season, Michael Jordan pointed into the crowd as a gesture of appreciation, which was met responsively by the adoring, chanting, swaying, singing, reveling mass.

This was from the heart, from the Bulls to Chicago and back.

As much as this 1992 championship was an invitation for the Bulls to join the league's Hall of Fame – for only three other franchises ever have won back-to-back titles – it was a union of a team and its city.

Chicago overcomes fire and flood; the Bulls overcome the challenges set before a champion.

Michael Jordan, the first back-to-back winner of the championship series' MVP award – unanimous both times – said many times during the season how difficult it was for him. But it was no less so for the Bulls, for champions are challenged every

By Sam Smith

game in the NBA and every day of their lives. They must restrain the fire of their competitors while maintaining their own cool demeanors.

The Bulls did both as impressively as it ever has been done.

They challenged immortality all season by shooting at the league single-season record for wins before settling for a fourth-best-ever 67 victories. They ripped off team-record winning streaks regularly, 14 in

November, 13 in January.

If gossip swirled on occasion, it was mostly the idol kind. The only reading they did was of their opponents, of the sag in the shoulders and the desperation, even fear, in the eyes. The Bulls' confidence remained sedative enough against fatigue and the wearing pressure of the marathon NBA season.

And they never sank in the sea of troubles.

Both Jordan and Scottie Pippen were All-Stars, and Phil Jackson was chosen to coach the best. Little did anyone know, he did that for 82 regular-season and 22 playoff games more than in that one All-Star game in February.

Hard to believe, the Bulls lost two of their first three games of the regular season. And there were hollow moments, like Jordan being ejected and sus-

NANCY STONE

pended after that triple overtime loss to the Jazz in Salt Lake City, plus blowing 20-point leads at home to the Orlando Magic and the Indiana Pacers.

But those moments were the exceptions. The 1991-92 season was as much a coronation as a celebration.

The Bulls finally silenced the hated Pistons so much that the rivalry didn't even seem to matter much anymore. They won more than 40 times during the season by margins of 10 points or more and recorded one of the largest spreads between points scored and yielded – the true margin of a team's dominance – in league history.

They were starting to walk with the giants.

For that's what they were. Jordan, the incomparable one who won his third MVP award and the continuing gasps of a nation. He and Pippen – the first choice among forwards – were both selected to join the elite 1992 U.S. Olympic basketball team. But there was Horace Grant, gaining his due as one of the league's best power forwards, virtually redefining the position with his speed, cunning and power.

There were Bill Cartwright and John Paxson, both having proved to be capable scorers who continually sacrificed their offense for the betterment of team play

Bill Cartwright gives a victory hug to teammates Craig Hodges and Bobby Hansen in the closing minutes of the NBA Finals.

NBA Playoffs MVP and Olympian Michael Jordan is swamped for autographs during a playoff visit to Portland.

preached by Jackson.

And there were the supporting players, every bit as important. That's why they give Academy Awards to the bit players, too.

B.J. Armstrong emerged as a scoring force off the bench, and Scott Williams took his place as a developing power player. Will Perdue, the fans' favorite, responded when he had to, as did three-peat three-point shooting champion Craig Hodges, Stacey King, Cliff Levingston and the new kid in the blocks, Bobby Hansen.

And when the playoffs came –

their crucible, really, for they were warned everywhere they'd never faced anything like this – they would truly never waver in bringing Chicago its first back-to-back title since the 1940-41 Bears. It was the first championship on local soil since the 1963 Bears and the first one in the Stadium in more than 50 years.

Yes, this was a team for the ages, sweeping through the Miami Heat, then defying the anger and hostility of the New York Knicks over seven games and the gutty Cleveland Cavaliers over six.

So on to their destiny they would march, to face the feared and fearsome Portland Trail Blazers, admired for their great talent and mastery of the Western Conference.

But they would fall, too, finally in six games, and ever so dramatically in the sixth as the Bulls came storming back from a record 15-point fourth-quarter deficit to win and share their talent and ability with all Chicago and to declare their dominance once and for all over the entire basketball world. ●

WARMUPS

*Michael Jordan struggles
with an image of perfection*

Be like Mike? Well, you can have it, said Michael Jordan, because it isn't all that much fun anymore.

"My situation is totally outrageous," he said about the heights his stardom has reached. "People ask me to explain it, and I can't. I don't know exactly what I did to put myself in this predicament, other than to be myself."

A "predicament" is as good a way as any for Jordan to describe his status as an American icon. Burden is another.

But there is no escaping the image he has carved during his eight-year career with the Bulls. An image that earns him $15 million to $20 million a year in endorsements.

By Melissa Isaacson

An image of all that is great in basketball and greater still in America.

An image, said Jordan, that has taken on a life of its own.

"It's like it is controlling its own self now," he said. "And I'm like this little machine that's got to direct it, so that it acts the way most people perceive it should act."

You wonder if there would have been a controversial bestseller, questions about his marketing decisions with Nike, uproar over his whereabouts when the rest of his world champion teammates visited President Bush and scrutiny of his golf companions if he did not set himself up to be the perfect athlete. The perfect man.

Jordan wonders, too.

DON BIERMAN

When he was drafted by the Bulls at age 22, Jordan said no one – not the team, not his agent, not his sponsors and certainly not himself – had any idea how high his star would rise.

"It's just one of those things that happened," he said. "And it shocked everybody. It's a hell of a burden, and it's one of those things I just stumbled into.

"Then you see people counting on you so much that you start to try to constantly maintain it, and that's when the pressure starts to mount. Suddenly, everything you do, you have to think, 'How is this going to be perceived?' "

One "perception" controversy involved huge golf gambling debts to two individuals of questionable character – one with a previous criminal record on drug charges, another man since slain.

And Jordan, who at first reacted defensively to the questions regarding his judgment and choice of friends, now kicks himself for getting involved in the first place.

Jordan had no idea how high his star would rise, he says. "It's just one of those things …"

"It was one of the most unusual situations I've ever been in," he said, "because I'm very cautious of people. But I put a lot of faith in third-party [introductions]. I probably shouldn't have, and it burned me."

With the media bearing down, Jordan could not have reacted any better. He was properly remorseful, took responsibility for his actions, apologized to his family, his teammates and his fans, and promised to be more careful in the future.

The "right" response.

"And you know what," he said, "it was just what I felt. … As I approached the situation, I just felt I had

to tell what was on my mind, which was an apology. To tell them how I felt about it and the embarrassment I encountered, and hopefully put it behind me.

"At some point in my life, I probably would have had to face it," he said. "Very few people go through their lifetimes without scars. And I went through a six- or seven-year period without them. Now I have a couple of scars, and I've got to mend them and keep moving on. The scars won't go away, but you know you're going to be a better person because of them."

To look at Jordan's face, smiling one moment, perplexed the next – he really could be the guy, even the kid, next door. And he feels that way. Sometimes.

"I tell my wife that I have a split personality," he said. "I lead two lives. Because in some ways, I'm projected to be a 38-, 39-year-old mature person who has experienced life to the fullest and now he's more or less settled down and focused on very conservative things.

"But the other side of me is a 29-year-old who never really got the chance to experience his success with friends and maybe do some of the crazy things that 27-, 28-, 29-year-old people will do. And sometimes I have those urges to do those things, but it can only be done in the privacy of the very small group of people who really know you as that 29-year-old person."

Does he, in some ways, wish he could always be his alter ego?

"You can't," he said, "because now what you see is what a nearly 30-year-old person has learned from it."

DON BIERMAN

Still, the idea of being a spokesman for his generation, a hero to children and a role model for his race frightens him, Jordan says, because frankly he's not ready for it.

"I don't think I've experienced life enough to voice so many opinions, and that's why I can't consider myself an ambassador for the league," he said.

"I think people want my opinion only because of the role-model image that has been bestowed on me. But that doesn't mean I've experienced all these things."

Ask him if it has all been worth it, and he goes back and forth.

"Everything seemed to snowball for the good," he said of his career. "From a financial situation, it's worth it. But away from that, it has been a burden to a certain extent.

"It caused extra pressure, but at the same time, it earned the respect and admiration of a lot of people. Everyone likes to be respected and admired."

And everyone, or so they say, wants to be like Mike.

Jordan smiles.

Jordan carries on an animated conversation with a referee (far left) as the Bulls huddle up during an April 3 game in Chicago.

"Pros and cons. The pros are, yeah, you sign autographs and maybe you get a free meal if you go to a restaurant, or people buy you drinks.

"But you also have to talk about being able to go to the restaurant, or a movie or shopping for Christmas or birthday presents without being bothered.

"It's not always fair." ●

A BANNER EVENING

Championship intensity remains as pageantry reigns opening night

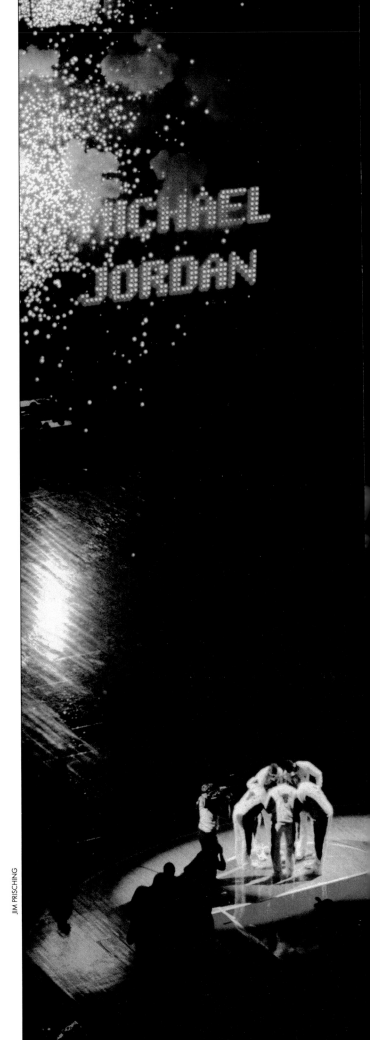

The stark, white world-championship banner seemed illuminated against the black rafters of Chicago Stadium, rotating slightly, almost haughtily, in its temporary position just off center court.

Amid a flurry of flashbulbs that lit up the darkened arena like a laser-light show, the banner had been hoisted, the Bulls Brothers disappeared into a vat of dry ice and the championship rings were distributed one by one as the fans gave each of their heroes his due on opening night of the 1991-92 season.

The basketball game that followed was as well-choreographed as the preceding pageantry, resulting in a 110-90 opening night wipeout of the Philadelphia 76ers. The outcome pleased coach Phil Jackson, who worried about a post-championship letdown.

"The game was featured in its greatest form, with the Bulls playing at championship intensity," said Jackson. "I was pleased most that we came out with intensity despite all the hoopla."

The Bulls would need all the intensity they could muster for the long season ahead.

— Melissa Isaacson

JIM PRISCHING

8

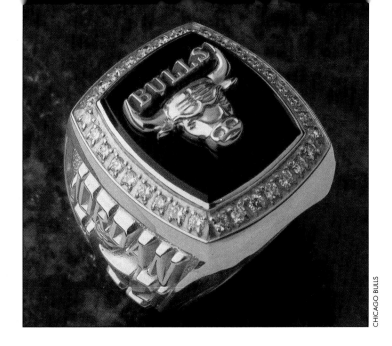

CHICAGO BULLS

THE CHAMPIONSHIP RING

Symbol of 1991 success designed to be as special as the season

Jerry Reinsdorf, managing partner of the Bulls, had this notion that the symbol of the Bulls' success – their 1991 championship ring – should be something more than the normal pedestrian designs.

"It always seemed to me that they looked like your average high school or fraternity ring," said Reinsdorf. "I wanted this to be a real piece of jewelry."

So Reinsdorf hired the experts in the field, Jostens, the company that made the size 23 Super Bowl ring that William Perry wears, the rings of 16 of the 25 Super Bowl winners and title rings for the Pistons, Lakers and Celtics and world heavyweight boxing champion Evander Holyfield.

Then Reinsdorf consulted another jewelry expert, who just happened to be his wife, Martyl. And this was not one of your wife-of-the-owner-decides-what-team-wears kind of things.

Martyl is a celebrated designer of cloisonne, which is an intricate ancient art that blends gold, silver and copper wire on enamel to form figurative pieces. A Japanese and Chinese history major in school, Martyl has designed pieces from adaptions of ancient Oriental and Greek legends.

Thus came the 14-karat-gold Bulls ring with the team's bull logo raised on a black onyx stone and surrounded by 30 small diamonds.

"It's a unique, distinctive design," said Jack Wheeler of Jostens. "It has a real European flair, and we feel the ring is a jumping-off point for future championship rings in all sports."

On one side of the ring is the player's or staff member's name, a depiction of the NBA championship trophy and the team's record in 1990-91, 61-21. The other side reports, "1991 World Champions," along with the NBA logo and the 15-2 Bulls' playoff record.

The rings were manufactured in the Jostens plant in Princeton, Ill., under the supervision of Martyl. She spent two days at the plant working with the company's design staff.

The largest ring went to Bill Cartwright, a size 14, and the smallest to B.J. Armstrong and Craig Hodges, both wearing size 9.

There was no shortage of rings. The Bulls handed out more than 100 rings – believed to be the most by an NBA champion – to the team, staff and office personnel.

– **Sam Smith**

9

STARTING LINEUP

MICHAEL JORDAN

A superstar's challenge:
Sometimes you have to face the fire

Michael Jordan once again lived up to his reputation as the greatest basketball player ever and took home his third Most Valuable Player award.

A basketball game in two scenes.

Scene One:

Derision is almost too subtle for the address, this being an in-your-face kind of place, so the Madison Square Garden menagerie gets style points for its sing-song mocking of Michael Jordan after he clanks the mother of all breakaway dunks off the back of the 7th Avenue rim just before halftime.

Bernie Lincicome
IN THE WAKE OF THE NEWS

"Myyy-kel, Myyy-kel," they chant, as they do for Darryl Strawberry when Darrr-yl comes back to town.

"Better eat your Wheaties," they suggest. "Myyy-kel. Myyy-kel."

Jordan will say later that he didn't notice, didn't

Michael Jordan

Position: Guard
Height: 6-6
Weight: 198 pounds
Birth date: 2/17/63
College: North Carolina
REGULAR-SEASON STATS

Games	80
Avg. minutes	38.8
Field goal pct.	.519
Free throw pct.	.832
3-point pct.	.270
Avg. rebounds	6.4
Avg. assists	6.1
Avg. steals	2.3
Scoring avg.	30.1

NANCY STONE

see the repeated replays on the scoreboard, forgot about the thing the moment after it happened.

"I guess I was overpumped," he will say.

Nothing the Knicks have done to this point has pleased their fans as much as Jordan's grand gaffe, but the Knicks take the freebie and begin to feed off their audience's delight, running off eight straight points.

Pat Riley, the Knicks coach, will later admit he felt the Knicks were now up 2-1 instead of down 1-2. A Jordan blooper messes with reality.

Scene two:

Fourth quarter. The Knicks have not dashed off as promised, but they have managed to cling and claw and stay in touch with the Bulls.

It is time for the game to be won. It is time for the series to be defined.

Jordan already has been leveled once trying to take the ball to the basket. Scottie Pippen and Jordan have been shooting jumpers, and doing it well, but this is becoming a male thing. Are the Bulls tough enough?

Jordan has the ball. "One of those inspirational plays," he will explain.

"A playoff play," Bulls coach Phil Jackson will say.

If his first step is quick enough, Jordan may be able to squeeze through between Xavier McDaniel and Patrick Ewing to the basket. Even so, Jordan is going to get hit.

"Sometimes you have to face the fire," Jordan will say.

Up goes Jordan. In come both McDaniel and Ewing in a vengeful vise. McDaniel catches Jordan in the face, blood spurts from Jordan's nose, the ball exits the bottom of the net, McDaniel and Ewing crash into each other and land in a heap, one on top of the other. Jordan will hover in triumph over Ewing, shaking his fist.

Jordan will shoot his free throw before having his nose packed to stop the bleeding. He will finish the game on one nostril.

The Knicks will not recover from this, not this day, not the next. Not when the series returns to Chicago for the last game. This one is over.

Myyy-kel. Michael.

Sometimes you have to face the fire. ●

13

SCOTTIE PIPPEN

The Bulls' second superstar: His game 'doesn't have any bounds'

Champion, Olympian, a star among stars. Scottie Pippen has become all of these. Now he stands on the verge of becoming perhaps the top star in the game – if not right now, then maybe in a year or two.

"He's as close to [Michael] Jordan right now as you can be," said Dallas coach Richie Adubato. "He's a star right there with Jordan."

"He has emerged as a superstar," said teammate John Paxson. "He's gotten to the point where he has a chance to be considered with the great ones."

Back-to-back championships have been sandwiched around Pippen's being the first forward selected for the U.S. team competing in the '92 Summer Olympics and his second All-Star game appearance in three years. Despite the accolades, Pippen thinks he still has a way to go.

"I don't feel like a star, not at all," said the 6-foot-8-inch, 225-pound forward. "I don't feel like I've reached my potential yet."

Bulls coach Phil Jackson does not disagree. "Scottie's game doesn't have any bounds," he said. "The big thing for Scottie was having confidence that he could hit the outside shot. Once he got that, the rest of his game filled in."

It all started to come together when Pippen made the All-Star team in 1990, and while he started slowly in 1990-91, his game broke out late in the season, not coincidentally when the Bulls broke out and galloped to an NBA title.

Pippen found himself a

national celebrity, featured in commercials and revered around the NBA. The Bulls rewarded him with a five-year, $18 million contract extension that will keep him with Chicago through the 1997-98 season.

"I know I've come a long way," Pippen said. "A lot has happened fast. … I'm taking the game a lot more seriously. I have a better feel for the game now. I'm at the stage where I've matured.

"I've been overshadowed by Michael in a lot of ways, so people have said it's tough to get to that position of recognition, but it's also been rewarding to have done so. I realize if I were on another team, I could be [the main guy], but I also get a lot of opportunities playing with Michael.

"I have a lot of confidence in myself now. There are a lot of things I want to do in this game. … but I can't talk about it. I have to just come out and do it."
– **Sam Smith and Melissa Isaacson**

Pippen broke out to stand as a star among stars during the Bulls' run to their first championship in 1991 after making the All-Star team for the first time in 1990.

MICHAEL MEINHARDT

14

Scottie Pippen

Position: Guard-forward
Height: 6-8
Weight: 225 pounds
Birth date: 9/25/65
College: C. Arkansas

REGULAR-SEASON STATS

Games	82
Avg. minutes	38.6
Field goal pct.	.506
Free throw pct.	.760
3-point pct.	.200
Avg. rebounds	7.7
Avg. assists	7.0
Avg. steals	1.9
Scoring avg.	21.0

HORACE GRANT

The new prototype: An agile player with a warrior's mentality

There is a twinkle in Horace Grant's eye that never seems to go away.

Whether he's joking with his teammates or explaining an off-night to the media, there is a certain something there that belies the man who straps on his goggles each night and tears down rebounds with fury.

Ask him about it and, as always, he laughs. With Grant, there is forever the attempt to put those around him at ease. To disarm even the occasional antagonist. To react to things around him as if it is for the very first time.

"I love to sit back and observe people and the things they do," said Grant. "I see the media always around Michael [Jordan] and the little things he does to keep from getting it blown out of proportion.

"That's a lot of pressure. And I want to stay looking young. I don't want to lose my hair or get gray at a young age."

And so he goes about his business as third chair to Jordan and

Grant isn't looking for stardom, he only wants respect for the accomplishments he has made.

MICHAEL MEINHARDT

Horace Grant	
Position: Forward	
Height: 6-10	
Weight: 220 pounds	
Birth date: 7/4/65	
College: Clemson	
REGULAR-SEASON STATS	
Games	81
Avg. minutes	35.3
Field goal pct.	.578
Free throw pct.	.741
3-point pct.	.000
Avg. rebounds	10.0
Avg. assists	2.7
Avg. steals	1.2
Scoring avg.	14.2

Scottie Pippen with a smile and a mission on his mind. If he can't be the most glamorous player in the league or the most publicized, Grant can be the hardest worker. That suits him fine.

From a player who many thought was not quite big enough or strong enough five years ago, the 6-foot-10, 220-pound Grant has become a pre-eminent power forward in the NBA, a player most teams covet.

"In grade school, high school and college, my body was that of a finesse player. But my mentality

was like a warrior," Grant said. "It was always like that."

When he was knocked around in practice as a rookie by Charles Oakley and told he would have to add bulk, Grant gladly accepted the challenge.

Grant added 20 pounds in bulk, and increased his bench press by 70 pounds and his squat by about 100 pounds. He improved his vertical jump by 2½ inches and his speed by about 5 percent.

"He's the new prototype of the power forward in this league," said assistant coach Johnny Bach. "Quick, agile, up the floor defensively, running the full floor. And he hasn't even touched his vast potential."

– Melissa Isaacson

17

The dream came true for Paxson in Game 5 of the Finals during the first championship run, when he scored 20 points.

JIM PRISCHING

JOHN PAXSON

A Bulls bit player who plays his role to perfection

The words resounded with numbing regularity throughout the NBA: The Bulls will not win a title until they get the right pieces around Michael Jordan.

"One of those pieces was point guard," remembers point guard John Paxson. "So it was like I had this thing attached to me."

He possessed an ego, as all accomplished performers do, but he could not rid himself of that stigma, would not rid himself of it until that night in Los Angeles. There, in the Fabulous Forum, John Paxson finally did shake free.

He shook free with a preternat- ural perfor- mance in Game 5 of the NBA Finals when he scored 20 points in the victory that would give the Bulls their long-coveted first title. He hit shots with all the regularity of a metronome, and when the game was over and the championship was won, he burst into the locker room and grabbed his wife tightly.

"This," he said to her in an uncharacteristic burst of emotion,

John Paxson	
Position: Guard	
Height: 6-2	
Weight: 185 pounds	
Birth date: 9/29/60	
College: Notre Dame	
REGULAR-SEASON STATS	
Games	79
Avg. minutes	24.6
Field goal pct.	.528
Free throw pct.	.784
3-point pct.	.273
Avg. rebounds	1.2
Avg. assists	3.1
Avg. steals	.62
Scoring avg.	7.0

"is what I worked so long for."

"For me," he remembers, "it was almost vindication. Not only to win it, but to be a big part of it.

"As a player, I guess you always dream that something like that is going to happen to you. As a kid, I always did that, but how many kids dream the same thing? For me, though," he said with a placid smile, "for me, though, the dream came true."

– Skip Myslenski

Cartwright understands that what the Bulls need most from him is his physical presence.

JIM PRISCHING

BILL CARTWRIGHT

'You've got to accept blows and you've got to give blows'

Bill Cartwright, at 7-1, is a 12-year NBA veteran with creaky knees, pointy elbows, spots of gray and a power game that, like it or not, has fully matured.

As the Bulls' starting center, Cartwright provides the brawn, the intimidating defense and invaluable NBA experience that enables him to know just how much he can get away with, and just what is expected of him.

"I think there's a certain attitude that you have to have to play center in this league," says Cartwright. "You've got to accept blows and you've got to give blows and you can't let it bother you.

"And certainly on this team you have to understand what your role is and be willing to play that role, and that's a big part of it, understanding what the team needs from you and going out and giving it to them."

Cartwright understands that what the Bulls need most from him is that physical presence. But don't confuse his style of play with his personality.

"It's not really Bill's nature ... to be rough and tumble, it's just a characteristic of his play," says assistant coach Tex Winter.

Cartwright says he's more comfortable as a starter. "I think I'm a geek-type of a guy," he says. "I like to come out of the gate. That's my favorite part of the game, the first part. I always think I'm ready to go. Some guys need a couple shots to get going. As soon as the game starts, I'm ready to play."

— Melissa Isaacson

Bill Cartwright	
Position: Center	
Height: 7-1	
Weight: 245 pounds	
Birth date: 7/30/57	
College: San Francisco	
REGULAR-SEASON STATS	
Games	64
Avg. minutes	23.0
Field goal pct.	.467
Free throw pct.	.604
3-point pct.	.000
Avg. rebounds	5.1
Avg. assists	1.4
Avg. steals	.34
Scoring avg.	8.0

THE BENCH

B.J. Armstrong shows he's more than the Bulls' heartthrob

CHUCK BERMAN

If Michael Jordan is the Sir Laurence Olivier of the NBA, then B.J. Armstrong must be its Luke Perry. The ubiquitous Jordan makes the cover of *Sports Illustrated* for the umpteenth time, while the fresh-faced Armstrong gets interviewed by *Seventeen*.

That's the way it is with Armstrong. The boyish looks, the nickname and the casual demeanor have helped make Benjamin Roy Armstrong something of a teen idol in Chicago.

Not exactly what he set out to accomplish, perhaps, but something that he accepts as "flattery" of the highest order. A glance in his mailbox tells the story.

"I haven't seen the other guys' mail, but I do seem to get a lot of fan mail, in particular, from a lot of girls and women," Armstrong said. "But I guess that's probably the business. I've never paid it any mind. I just concentrate on becoming the best basketball player I can."

In his third season in the NBA, Armstrong

B.J. Armstrong	
Position: Guard	
Height: 6-2	
Weight: 175 pounds	
Birth date: 9/9/67	
College: Iowa	
REGULAR-SEASON STATS	
Games	82
Avg. minutes	22.9
Field goal pct.	.481
Free throw pct.	.806
3-point pct.	.402
Avg. rebounds	1.8
Avg. assists	3.2
Avg. steals	.56
Scoring avg.	9.9

Armstrong sees his role clearly: "My job is to be ready when Phil calls on me. I'm a reserve, and I understand that. I'll be there."

20

came to what some consider a critical juncture in his career. He saw his playing time increase slightly from 21 to 23 minutes a game in 1991-92 and his scoring average rise from 8.8 to 9.9 points a game. He could start for many other NBA teams, but was content to back up John Paxson and await his turn in the spotlight.

More important to Armstrong, however, was that coach Phil Jackson frequently left him in the lineup at the conclusion of games.

Though he didn't replace Paxson as the team's regular starting point guard, Armstrong took on a much higher profile on the bench. He even felt the need to defend himself and his peers after coach Phil Jackson and Jordan both criticized the bench for lack of production in Game 4 of the Eastern Conference finals vs. Cleveland.

"We're all adults," Armstrong responded. "If they have a knock against the bench, then they should come and talk to the guys on the bench, and let's work it out rather than to try to point fingers at people."

It was an uncharacteristically strong statement from Armstrong, who has a knack for saying just the right thing.

"I'm not saying that was correct, and I'm not saying they were correct in saying that. Maybe it was just to motivate us. Who knows? It was nothing personal, not a personal attack. It was just something that I felt needed to be said. It didn't seem to harm the team or anything, and I know we'll just move on.

"My job is to be ready when Phil calls on me," Armstrong said. "I'm a reserve, and I understand that. I'll be there. Hopefully, it'll be on the floor."
— Paul Sullivan

Will Perdue (above) and Stacey King (below) come off the bench to spell Bill Cartwright depending on whom coach Phil Jackson feels suits the situation.

Will Perdue

Position: Center
Height: 7-0
Weight: 240 pounds
Birth date: 8/29/65
College: Vanderbilt

REGULAR-SEASON STATS	
Games	77
Avg. minutes	13.1
Field goal pct.	.547
Free throw pct.	.495
3-point pct.	.500
Avg. rebounds	4.1
Avg. assists	1.0
Avg. steals	.21
Scoring avg.	4.5

Stacey King

Position: Forward-center
Height: 6-11
Weight: 230 pounds
Birth date: 1/29/67
College: Oklahoma

REGULAR-SEASON STATS	
Games	79
Avg. minutes	16.1
Field goal pct.	.506
Free throw pct.	.753
3-point pct.	.400
Avg. rebounds	2.6
Avg. assists	.97
Avg. steals	.27
Scoring avg.	7.0

21

NANCY STONE

Position: Guard
Height: 6-2
Weight: 190 pounds
Birth date: 6/27/60
College: Long Beach St.

REGULAR-SEASON STATS	
Games	56
Avg. minutes	9.9
Field goal pct.	.384
Free throw pct.	.941
3-point pct.	.375
Avg. rebounds	.43
Avg. assists	.96
Avg. steals	.25
Scoring avg.	4.3

The Bulls bench is one of the most versatile in the NBA – each man fits a specific role. Craig Hodges (left), a two-time winner of the NBA's 3-point shootout, provides potent long-range shooting. Cliff Levingston (below) can spell Horace Grant at power forward or fill the void at small forward when Scottie Pippen takes a breather.

Cliff Levingston

Position: Forward
Height: 6-8
Weight: 210 pounds
Birth date: 1/4/61
College: Wichita State

REGULAR-SEASON STATS	
Games	79
Avg. minutes	12.9
Field goal pct.	.498
Free throw pct.	.625
3-point pct.	.166
Avg. rebounds	2.9
Avg. assists	.84
Avg. steals	.34
Scoring avg.	3.9

ED WAGNER

22

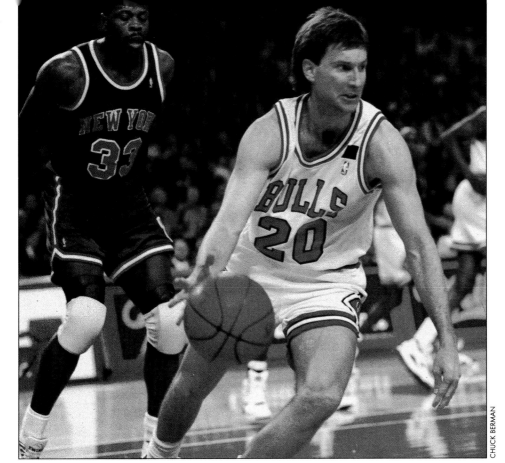

CHUCK BERMAN

Bobby Hansen	
Position: Guard	
Height: 6-6	
Weight: 195 pounds	
Birth date: 1/18/61	
College: Iowa	
REGULAR-SEASON STATS	
Games	68
Avg. minutes	11.9
Field goal pct.	.444
Free throw pct.	.364
3-point pct.	.259
Avg. rebounds	1.1
Avg. assists	1.0
Avg. steals	.39
Scoring avg.	2.5

Bobby Hansen (left), who joined the team early in the season, is used mainly as a defensive specialist when called in off the bench.

In only his second year, Scott Williams (right) was an imposing force under the basket, providing strength and aggressiveness as a reserve at both center and power forward.

Scott Williams	
Position: Center	
Height: 6-10	
Weight: 230 pounds	
Birth date: 8/21/68	
College: North Carolina	
REGULAR-SEASON STATS	
Games	63
Avg. minutes	11.0
Field goal pct.	.483
Free throw pct.	.649
3-point pct.	.000
Avg. rebounds	3.9
Avg. assists	.79
Avg. steals	.21
Scoring avg.	3.4

MICHAEL MEINHARDT

PHIL JACKSON

'Best coach in Bulls history' reaps the rewards of the championship years

DON BIERMAN

Phil Jackson, considered by many to be the best coach in Bulls history, is reaping the rewards of that distinction: the best coaching contract in franchise history.

A three-year extension, estimated to be worth about $2.5 million, will take effect after the 1992-93 season, the final year of Jackson's original four-year contract. He earned about $325,000 for the 1991-92 season.

"I've been associated with about every one of them [Bulls coaches]," said general manager Jerry Krause, who worked for the club when Dick Motta and Doug Collins, among others, directed the team. "Without question, Phil has been the best coach in team history."

Jackson's deal is believed to be the richest Jerry Reinsdorf has ever given a coach or manager as chairman of the Bulls and the White Sox.

Jackson, who has the best winning percentage of any coach in NBA history, raised the possibility he might leave the game, at least temporarily, when his extension expires, which would coincide with the final year of Michael Jordan's contract.

"At some point, I think a coach needs a sabbatical. You do get burned out. One hundred games a year is a lot of coaching, and you must rejuvenate yourself. That's why we anticipated this as a three-year deal."

The Bulls had offered him a four-year extension, but Jackson said: "We felt seven years of intensity of coaching an NBA club is really up to a limit. Then you've got to stop and evaluate where you are as a coach and where you are in your personal life."

In 1987, Krause brought Jackson to the Bulls as an assistant coach from what appeared to be an exile in the Continental Basketball Association for his iconoclastic ways as an NBA player.

"I think Phil is one of the best coaches in the NBA right now," Krause said. "And I think the day is going to come when everyone in this league says Phil is the best coach in the NBA. There's no one we'd rather have coaching this ball club.

"Phil gives us the stability we were seeking. We were looking for an outstanding coach to go along with the young players so this team could be a contender for years to come."

Since taking over for the fired Collins in July 1989, Jackson's win total is second among Bulls coaches only to Motta, who guided the team for eight seasons. Jackson led the team to the seventh game of the 1990 Eastern Conference championship and then, in 1991, to its first NBA title.

Bulls coach Phil Jackson (above) talks strategy with Michael Jordan. Jackson (right) reacts to a humorous question at the press conference announcing his new contract.

"Three years ago," said Krause, "a lot of you guys were jumping on me pretty good when we made this move. So it's gratifying for me to see what Phil has done."

– Sam Smith

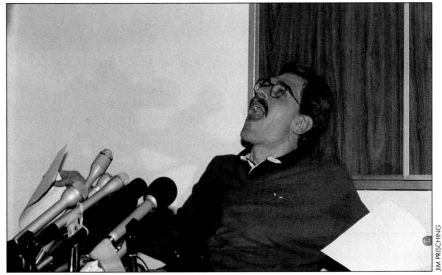

25

CHARLES CHERNEY

FIRST HALF

The regular season: 'Everyone comes at you so hard every night'

There are no regular-season games when you're defending an NBA title.

There are 82 games filled with playoff intensity before the playoffs even begin, with each and every opponent itching for the ultimate conquest, to beat the best.

The defending champs catch no one on an off night. On the road, there is an ambush waiting at every stop. That is why there were only three teams in recent history to successfully defend an NBA title.

That is why winning a franchise record 67 games – fourth-most in NBA history – was so amazing for the Chicago Bulls in the 1991-92 regular season that was anything but regular.

"Everyone comes at you so hard every night," guard John Paxson said. "All you can do is absorb their best shot, then counter with your own and hope it's good enough."

Most of the time it was. When the Bulls punched the accelerator, the car responded, speeding out of trouble like one of Michael Jordan's sports cars.

The Bulls won a team-record 14 consecutive games early in the season. They never lost more than two straight or more than four in any month. And, naturally, Jordan won his sixth consecutive scoring title.

The season might have begun with a cloud overhead – fallout from a bestseller and Jordan's Presidential Snub – but that was merely a shadow from the spotlight beneath which they performed so well during this second championship season. •

THE KO DEFENSE

Furious late-game frenzy often puts away Bulls' opponents

They have been likened to high-speed engines, prized canines and killer sharks.

Their ability to time their attack, to strike and to destroy is widely feared and makes them sound like any number of dangerous forces, from mammal to military.

In a sport so often dictated by rallies and streaks, the Bulls are already the undisputed champions at putting a game away. They have demonstrated, like no other team, the ability to outscore opponents in large, quick, lethal doses.

"There are times when four times down the court you score and your opponent may score, too," said coach Phil Jackson. "But what we're able to do is put together a flurry, kind of like a knockout punch in a boxing match."

The list of KO victims goes on and on, good teams and bad, distinguishing the Bulls in a unique but very significant category.

"The great Celtics teams used to do that, blow you out with one streak" said Pat Williams, general manager of the Orlando Magic. "You knew it was coming; it was just a question of when and if you

The big surge

Late-game scoring spurts by the Bulls in games that they won:

DATE	OPPONENT	SURGE SCORE	QUARTER	FINAL SCORE
Nov. 9	Orlando	28-12	3rd	107-76
Nov. 12	Detroit	14-0	3rd	110-93
Nov. 13	Charlotte	29-9	4th	117-95
Nov. 26	L.A. Clippers	49-17	3rd-4th	116-79
Nov. 30	Sacramento	22-9 9-1	3rd 4th	118-102
Dec. 13	New York	11-2	3rd	99-89
Dec. 14	Washington	12-2	3rd	111-100
Dec. 20	New Jersey	24-6	2nd-3rd	115-98
Dec. 21	Atlanta	11-1	4th	104-93
Jan. 10	Utah	15-3	3rd	105-90
Jan. 25	Houston	15-4	3rd	114-100
Feb. 11	New Jersey	14-2	4th	133-113
March 5	Minnesota	18-0	3rd	113-100
March 11	Boston	18-3	3rd	119-85
March 14	Orlando	22-4	3rd	112-96
March 16	Miami	18-5	3rd	116-100
March 17	New Jersey	18-0	4th	90-79
April 17	Atlanta	15-3	3rd	121-95

could withstand it. It's the sign of a great team, and it's certainly the case with the Bulls."

The game-breaking runs are almost always keyed by the defense, led by the gambling duo of Michael Jordan and Scottie Pippen.

"What sets them apart is that

they have two of the biggest stars in the game who are first-team all-pros both offensively and defensively," said Golden State coach Don Nelson.

What makes Jordan and Pippen even more dangerous is their support system. "They're buoyed by what the defense behind them will do," Jackson said. "Our interior defense of [Bill] Cartwright and [Horace] Grant know how to cover for them. [John] Paxson knows how to hold up the timing for a guard."

It can be as much as a steal or as little as a nod of the head that gets them going. That thought sends shudders through opposing coaches.

"Their defense is so terrific already," said Utah coach Jerry Sloan, "that when they decide to step it up a notch, they can annihilate you. If you panic in that situation, you're in trouble, and most teams panic."

But it has backfired at times. Reserve center Will Perdue expressed concern that the Bulls might become too reliant on the third-quarter surge.

"We have enough quality personnel to do it whenever we want,

but the thing is, if we keep up that attitude, it's going to catch up to us," Perdue said. "There's going to be a game where we just kind of go through the motions and then say, 'OK, let's tighten the screws,' and it's not going to be there."

So is it a good habit or a bad one?

"I think it's a good habit," Jordan said. "It's not that we have relaxed in the first half and pushed ourselves in the second, necessarily. But in the first half, you have a chance to evaluate the opponent."

Statistically, the Bulls actually have held their opponents to fewer points in the first and second quarters, but the biggest point differential has come in the third quarter. Most would agree it only makes sense.

For one thing, the starters play more minutes in the first and third quarters. And it's only natural the intensity level in a 48-minute game would be held in reserve for key periods – most often in the final half in the NBA.

"The third period can make you or break you in this league," Stacey King said. "Usually the team that starts out hot [in the second half] has the best chance of winning the game. . . . The third quarter is the key."

– **Melissa Isaacson**

The defensive intensity of Scottie Pippen and the Bulls often causes other teams to panic.

BEATING THE BAD BOYS

Pistons' intimidation no longer works on Bulls

'They're not as 'bad' as they used to be."

That was Scottie Pippen's pronouncement after Chicago drubbed the Detroit Pistons 103-85 in the final game of the regular season series between the two rivals. The Bulls dominated, winning four of the five games, including three home wins by an average of 20 points. But each was an intense, physical battle.

Nov. 12

Yeah, yeah, sure. This game was no big deal.

So, uh, what exactly was that third quarter all about this night at the Stadium?

Those certainly looked like late-season shoves by Isiah Thomas. Sure appeared to be playoff-caliber kicks by Bill Laimbeer.

The Bulls administered a 110-93 pasting of the kind impossible without some good old-fashioned dislike and more than a little desire.

"This was like the same atmosphere as the playoffs," Michael Jordan said. "It has been, and always will be, a war."

Jan. 19

This time, only the fans left before the final buzzer. The Detroit Pistons stayed put.

And they didn't like what they saw.

"We are not intimidated by this team anymore," said Jordan.

It wasn't any easier for the Bulls. In fact, their 87-85 victory over the Pistons at the Palace was undoubtedly one of the hardest-earned of the season and comparable to any playoff game in terms of intensity and emotion. It featured three technicals and two scuffles in the first half alone.

Jan. 24

This was a game for creative headline writers, cagey photographers and those with a sense of the surreal.

It was certainly not for the Detroit Pistons, who would just

as soon read about power outages as opposed to any details about the 117-93 shellacking they took from the Bulls.

A blackout at the Stadium gave an eerie quality to the first quarter. The lights were at full strength by the second quarter, but things didn't fully return to normal until the third. That's when the Bulls, as they customarily do, turned up the juice.

"It was an unusual game," said coach Phil Jackson.

"Bizarre," is how Detroit coach Chuck Daly described the evening, and that seemed a closer fit.

Feb. 25

For one night, anyway, an icy February evening when National Basketball Association teams are forgiven for going through the motions, the Detroit Pistons relived their past.

Once again, they were the aggressors capable of not just throwing a scare into their Central Division rival Bulls, not just living on pride and emotion, but of rising to the level of the best.

On this night, Dennis Rodman wagged his finger, Bill Laimbeer threw his weight around and John Salley went to the free-throw line in the closing minutes.

And they all got away with it, much to the delight of the frenzied Palace crowd.

Jordan's last-second 15-footer glanced off the front end of the rim and into the crowd below as the buzzer sounded on this 108-106 Detroit victory.

April 19

Excuse the Bulls' restraint after completing the team's most successful regular season and the fourth-best in National Basketball Association history. See, it only hurts when they laugh.

Feeling the strain of an 82-game season, their 103-85 defeat of the Pistons in a typically physical Bulls-Pistons game at the Stadium was marred by an injury to Jordan.

Jordan came down hard after his first shot of the day, twisting his left side and lower back and sustaining a moderate muscle strain.

"This [game] was a great culmination to a terrific season," said Jackson, whose team tied a club record for best home mark at 36-5, set in the 1989-90 season. "This was a finale that obviously deserved a curtain call if any one did."

— Melissa Isaacson

Scott Williams and the Bulls felt the momentum shift after their romp over the Pistons in mid-April.

CHARLES CHERNEY

SEASON ON THE BRINK

Remembering 10 key games in a franchise-best regular season

o letdown. No dissension. No problem.

The fireworks started long before opening night for this record-setting Bulls team. When Michael Jordan skipped a preseason outing at George Bush's place and a best-selling book made the rounds, some skeptics expected the Bulls to suffer from defending champonitis.

No such luck for Bulls opponents. Here are 10 games that marked a franchise-best 67-15 season:

Nov. 1 vs. Philadelphia

Opening night, complete with a Chicago Stadium love-in, rings for everyone and a 110-90 wipeout of the 76ers.

Let the record show that the Bulls' first basket was scored by Horace Grant at 11:03 of the first quarter. The first floor burn was taken by Scottie Pippen at the 9:07 mark.

The Bulls erase memories of last year's season-opening defeat to the Sixers at the Stadium.

Nov. 5 vs. Golden State

The Bulls drop to 1-2 after losing 118-110 to the Warriors at the

By Bob Condor and Melissa Isaacson

Stadium, blowing a nine-point lead with what Grant calls a "nightmare" fourth quarter.

It is announced after the game that Craig Hodges will undergo arthroscopic surgery to repair torn cartilage in his left knee, knocking him out of the bench rotation for six weeks. This development, combined with John Paxson's injured left foot, prompts some fans to wonder whether the team should have traded Dennis Hopson to Sacramento for Bobby Hansen the previous day.

The fretting was unfounded. Paxson's foot healed quickly enough, and coach Phil Jackson's club subsequently reeled off 14 straight wins.

Nov. 12 vs. Detroit

In the first meeting between the bitter rivals since last year's Bulls sweep in the Eastern Conference finals, the Bulls administer a 110-93 pasting of the not-so-Bad Boys at the Stadium.

The Bulls, who come out of the locker room at halftime leading by three, begin the second half with a 14-0 run and enter the fourth leading by 22.

"Every time we play," said Pippen, "we expect high intensity and a playoff atmosphere. We don't want to lose these games. They stay with you awhile."

Dec. 25 vs. Boston

With a national TV audience looking on, the Bulls play their Scrooge act to the hilt with a 121-99 victory that isn't as close as the final score. Jordan scores just 14 points, his lowest output since November 1990.

Pippen has a game-leading 27 points, B.J. Armstrong scores 18 and Grant gets 17 points and 12 rebounds as six Bulls – including three reserves – finish in double figures.

As surprising as Jordan's 14 are Larry Bird's eight points. "I guess it didn't turn out to be as advertised: Bird vs. Jordan," Jordan quipped.

Jan. 19 at Detroit

The Bulls' 87-85 victory at the Palace is undoubtedly one of the hardest-earned of the season.

"We are not intimidated by this team anymore," said Jordan.

The Bulls trail for most of the fourth quarter, only to once again pull off the critical steal (by Jordan), the crucial three-pointers (by Paxson and Pippen) and the second-effort rebounds (by Grant, Bill Cartwright and Cliff Levingston).

Feb. 3 at Utah

For suspense, few games in this supreme regular season could rank with this late-night affair for Chicago fans. A triple-overtime Jazz victory doesn't end until Jordan, who forces the second overtime with a three-pointer and then fails to clinch the game in the second overtime by missing a pair of free throws, is ejected for cursing at and bumping referee Tommie Wood after Wood called him for a foul on Jeff Malone with a half-second left.

Malone converts the technical free throw and two more to provide the final 126-123 outcome in what some experts say could have been a preview of the NBA Finals.

Feb. 17 vs. Cleveland

From the Cavaliers' side of the basketball universe, the Bulls have this 113-112 loss coming. It is sealed on an errant last-second jumper by Pippen, snapping a 12-game losing streak to the Bulls as well as breaking Chicago's string of 14 straight victories at the Stadium.

"We knew sooner or later we would beat this team," said John "Hot Rod" Williams. "Tonight we just outplayed them."

March 1 vs. Portland

This 111-91 victory at the Stadium comes at the tail end of a three-game eastern trip for the Blazers.

Even so, these are still the Portland Trail Blazers, they of the most-athletic-ability-in-the-league albatross. And this does signify a sweep for the Bulls over the team voted most likely to meet them in the playoffs for two years running.

The Bulls lead by 15 at the half after holding the Blazers to 17 second-quarter points, then raise the edge to 24 early in the third and to 29 before the carnage is through.

They force the Blazers into 23 turnovers translating into 25 points and hold a team averaging 47 percent from the field to 31 percent in the first and 37 percent for the game.

March 3 vs. Indiana

"Hey, All-Star. Hey, Olympian. Don't shoot it short, now. You're the big superstar." That's what Reggie Miller says to Pippen as the Bulls forward stands at the free-throw line with 2.2 seconds left.

Two free throws would have tied the score. Instead, in as unlikely a turnabout as you're likely to see from this Bulls team in the Stadium, Pippen kicks the ball into the stands after missing his first attempt, and the Bulls succumb 103-101.

The Bulls blow a 22-point first-quarter lead.

April 19 vs. Detroit

The defending champs finish the fourth-best regular season in NBA history by drubbing the Pistons 103-85 without Grant.

The Bulls win their seventh straight against Detroit at home.

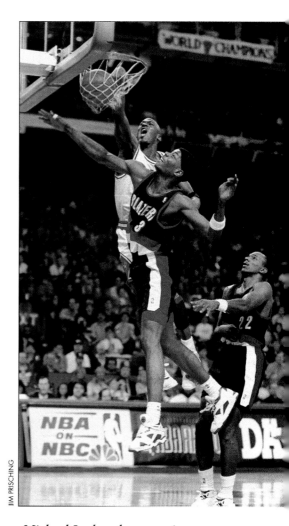

JIM PRISCHING

Michael Jordan slams one in against Portland's Cliff Robinson in a convincing March 1 victory at the Stadium.

They also complete their five-game season series at 4-1, including three victories at home by an average of 20 points.

"I guess you could call it sending a message," said Pippen. "This was a game we wanted to win and show that we're serious. It was a nice way to start building momentum and turning up the heat for the playoffs." ●

(Sam Smith contributed to this story)

HALFTIME

Tradition-rich Chicago Stadium lacks the frills but not the thrills

The outside is so drab and the inside too dark. The hallways are particularly dreary. Yet on game night, it is a delightful place to be.

The energy inside could light the city. If home is really where the heart is, then creaky Chicago Stadium is a mansion in disguise. The Bulls adore it.

The seats are wooden, the aisles narrow and the stairways endless. The locker rooms are small and outdated. The music still comes from an organ, 4,000 pipes with the power of 25 brass bands.

Opened on St. Patrick's Day in 1929, the Stadium today is a relic, missing all the amenities associated with the modern arenas of big-league sports. There are no elevators for convenience, no luxury suites for corporate execs and their customers, no outside fountains to entice people in.

What there is, is some wonderful tradition.

"I love the place," Michael Jordan says. "It's old-fashioned. It's history."

There have been heavyweight title fights, political conventions, wakes, track meets, auto races and Elvis concerts at Chicago Stadium. And now there are back-to-back NBA titles.

For opponents, it is annoying, dreadful and sometimes intimidating, especially when another sellout

Chicago Stadium has been the site of many special events, but nothing compares to two NBA titles.

MICHAEL MEINHARDT

34

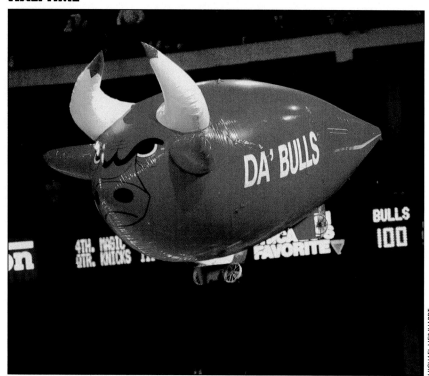

crowd lives up to its reputation as the loudest in the league. The metal roof reflects all noise back to the floor.

It can energize the Bulls and demoralize opponents.

When the lights go off, the spotlights appear and the pre-game introductions begin with "And now, the starting lineup for *your* Chicago Bulls …" people scream. Jordan is introduced last, but by then the roar is so deafening, no one really hears his name. They only see him materialize magically at midcourt.

Despite the charm, the end is near and obvious by the construction across the street of the new Stadium. Yet there are two more seasons to come at Chicago Stadium – still plenty of time to enjoy. ●

If the deafening noise in Chicago Stadium isn't enough to intimidate the other team, then maybe Da Bulls blimp will do the job. Benny the Bull and the Luvabulls add to the Stadium excitement when they take the floor during timeouts to entertain the crowd.

Chicago fans (above) count down the closing seconds of another Bulls' victory.

Bulls coach Phil Jackson (right) finds a quiet spot down below in Chicago Stadium to look over final game statistics.

SECOND HALF

A playoff walk in the park

becomes a race past the muggers

The road to the NBA Finals began like a Sunday drive down a freshly paved superhighway. Without warning, it became car trouble at midnight in an unfamiliar city.

The Bulls needed only cruise control in the opening sweep of the Miami Heat, as Michael Jordan had his way with the playoff neophytes, entertaining everyone with scoring bursts of 46 and 56 points.

They needed studded snow tires, four-wheel drive and a plow out front to fight past the New York Knicks in a seven-game second round that often looked like the Bad Boys of Detroit had returned for a curtain call. There were head butts, forearms and nasty words exchanged. Chicago's high-powered offense was forced to trudge through the mud.

The six-game third round against Cleveland included an embarrassing 26-point debacle at Chicago Stadium, the Bulls' worst home loss since 1985.

Clearly, the road was not as smooth as everyone expected. The walk in the park became a race past the muggers. The Bulls advanced, but they were not unscathed. ●

MIAMI THRICE

The Heat turn it on, but it isn't enough as the Bulls sweep

The Heat tried, they really did.

In its initiation to the NBA playoff world, Miami fought the Bulls every step of the way in their first-round series. But even a defiant stand by the Heat in front of the home crowd in Game 3 proved to be much too little and far too late.

A 113-94 victory in Game 1 achieved with only marginal satis-faction is not a luxury most teams enjoy. But for the Bulls, beating the Heat in the opener – behind a generous 46-point push from Michael Jordan and support from Will Perdue – gave them a strong sense the best was still ahead.

"It was just like the finals against the Lakers [in 1991] when we were amazed we had the opportunity to win the first game when nobody played particularly well," Jordan said. "And from that point on, we were able to dominate."

Coach Phil Jackson called it Jordan's "special time of the season."

"Michael kept us in there until we settled down," Jackson said. "We were very nervous about this game. The suspense of the play-offs was laboring in our minds."

The game turned, as it did so often for the Bulls during the regular season, in the third quarter. They turned a seven-point halftime lead to 14 at the end of three with deadly shooting and an improved defensive effort.

From there, it was simply a matter of grinding it out. And the Bulls, thanks to a 16-point, 10-rebound effort by Perdue, even made that look pretty.

This was the Bulls' personality that scared the shorts off most of the NBA teams for a good part of the season. They clamped on their customary defensive vise, taking a 12-point lead to rev up the crowd and gain a sense of control they would not relinquish.

While Miami may have surprised Chicago in the opener, Game 2 was a rude awakening for the Heat – 120-90.

"We're finding out what world champions are made of," said Heat coach Kevin Loughery. "We're finding out what it takes at this level, and how hard it is to get there."

Going into Game 3 on the ropes, Miami could only hope that the home crowd would exhort them to a higher level. It almost worked.

The Heat led by 18 in the first quarter and stayed in the hunt – three down with 11 seconds to go – until the bitter end of the Bulls' 119-114 victory. It took 56 points from Jordan and 31 from Pippen to sew up the series.

– **Melissa Isaacson**

The Bulls snuffed out the Heat, but not without a valiant fight from the young Miami team.

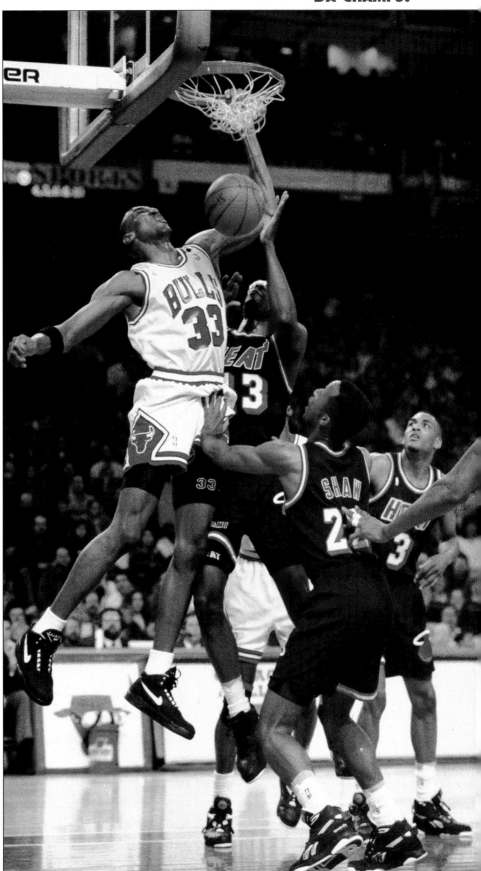

MICHAEL MEINHARDT

ED WAGNER

KNICKS, CUTS AND BRUISES

Riley's misfits come in clanking and rattling, and turn the Bulls into stammering, timid victims

This is only going to get uglier – and not just because the further adventures of the Bulls and Them moves next to the Big Litter for a weekend of assumable hostility. The only chance the Knicks have of beating the Bulls is more of the same.

And that is to make basketball into a tractor pull. Or mud wrestling.

There the Bulls were, the shining ideal of elegant and energetic basketball, princes with wings. And here come the Knicks with their bolts showing, clanking and rattling like so many spare parts, not merely annoying the Bulls, not just taking one of two in Chicago, but turning the Bulls themselves into stammering, timid victims.

"We're just not playing the same as we were last year at this time," Michael Jordan said. "We've got to struggle to find it."

This comes, of course, from the

Bernie Lincicome
IN THE WAKE OF THE NEWS

winner, though only on the scoreboard. In all other terms – rebounds, want to, floor burns – the Knicks were better again.

So, the Bulls won Game 2. What is more significant is that the Bulls did nothing to discourage the Knicks from thinking they can win again.

"Not one player is satisfied to come out of here with a split when we had a chance to win," said Knicks coach Pat Riley, adding the warning: "And now, to New York."

The Knicks have made this series dead even, not merely mathematically, but on the floor and in the heads of the Bulls.

This is sudden and disarming for a team so used to having everything its way.

"They've got us playing their stand-still game," admitted Phil Jackson, the Bulls coach.

Jackson blames, or credits, the offi-

Stacey King begins the celebration in the Bulls' decisive victory over the Knicks in Game 7 of the Eastern Conference semifinals. Scott Williams keeps his composure as the action continues.

cials for keeping the game floor-bound and half-court. But the Knicks can share, for they are using the only effective weapon they have: their complete lack of skill.

Aside from Patrick Ewing, who is containable, the Knicks cannot shoot, cannot run, cannot handle the ball without making a wish first.

The Knicks have cluttered the aesthetics of a lovely game, as *déclassé* as dropping a lug nut into the *créme brûlée*.

They are not just drawing a mustache on the Mona Lisa, they

are adding an eye patch and scars.

They have turned Jordan into Adrian Dantley, putting him back-up to the basket, turning, fading, shooting.

The Knicks have reduced Scottie Pippen to invisibility, though Pippen also has the excuse of an ouchy ankle.

Since only results matter, Xavier McDaniel is clearly outplaying Pippen.

The Knicks have so altered the Bulls' way of doing things that in Game 2, Jordan Time was turned over to B.J. Armstrong, or rather

Armstrong took it, having the fourth quarter of his life and the lives of Armstrongs yet unborn.

The Bulls allowed the Knicks to go home thinking more of themselves than logic and pedigree should allow.

If brother Dominique is the Human Highlight Film, Gerald Wilkins is a Small Appliance Repair Video.

They're all named Greg Anthony Mason or Mark Jackson Starks. Who knows?

But they've got the Bulls playing like a team that won't take a dare. ●

Game 1
Knicks   94
Bulls   89
Knicks lead series, 1-0

They were coming to Chicago to win, the New York Knicks insisted before this Eastern Conference semifinal series began, and it was anything but bravado.

It was jarring truth in the form of a grinding defense and an honest night's work by a team gliding along on the optimism from recent success.

Patrick Ewing, quieted by center Bill Cartwright in the first half, poured in 28 of his 34 points in the second half and carried the Knicks with 16 in the fourth as the Bulls could only watch their home-court advantage melt away.

The Bulls, down 10 points early in the fourth quarter, rode a 13-0 run to take the lead, 82-79, but the lead never got beyond one from then on, and with Ewing's 12-foot jumper after a drive across the middle at the 33-second mark, it was gone for good.

"We came to play," said Knicks coach Pat Riley. "I thought coming in that if there was ever a game to steal, this could be it."

It was the Knicks' first victory against the Bulls in their last 15 tries, and the first in their last 18 at the Stadium.
                      – Melissa Isaacson

Bill Cartwright was one of many Bulls who took it on the chin during the rugged Eastern Conference semifinals.

NANCY STONE

47

Xavier McDaniel passes out of a jam, but the Knicks come up short.

GAME 2
Bulls	86
Knicks	78

Series tied, 1-1

B.J. Armstrong saved the Bulls from some serious soul-searching as he scored 18 points on 7-for-10 shooting, including eight points in the fourth quarter.

The Knicks cut a 12-point, fourth-quarter deficit to six in a little less than a minute, and eventually to three at the 5:26 mark.

With the Stadium faithful desperately urging on the Bulls, Michael Jordan scored on a jumper, then Armstrong scooped up a loose ball at midcourt, dribbled straight to the hoop, then pitched the ball back to Horace Grant, who slammed it home.

The basket gave the Bulls a 77-70 lead with 4:15 left. The Knicks cut it to 79-78 with 2:05 left, but a short jumper by Armstrong gave the Bulls a three-point cushion at 1:40. The Bulls didn't look back as they went on to even up the series, 1-1, with an eight-point victory.

GAME 3
Bulls	94
Knicks	86

Bulls lead series, 2-1

Chicago's seventh consecutive victory against the Knicks at Madison Square Garden showed signs that the "real" Bulls were emerging. For instance:

• Pippen's 26 points on 7-of-12 shooting.

• Horace Grant's 10 points and 13 rebounds.

ED WAGNER

• Jordan's 32 points, nine rebounds and first and second dunks of the series.

The game's highlight, however, came with four minutes left in the first half. Captured and recaptured by every television camera in the place, Michael Jordan missed a breakaway dunk.

"I just tried to dunk it too hard," Jordan said of the attempted one-handed tomahawk, which bounced off the back of the rim and landed somewhere near the upper concourse. "I was very intense … and I was trying to take the rim down."

GAME 4
Knicks   93
Bulls   86
Series tied, 2-2

No open wounds this time. No mortal ones either. Just bruised egos, checked anger and a lot of frustration.

The Knicks took Round 4 in this first-team-to-90 competition, outmuscling the Bulls and sending the series back to Chicago with a tenor that was decidedly in favor of New York.

The Bulls' inability to play the Knicks' game and unwillingness to accept that fact resulted in a beating on the boards and the ejection of coach Phil Jackson.

New York's Xavier McDaniel scored 10 of his team-high 24 points during a 10½-minute span without Ewing, inspiring his teammates to a level of defensive intensity that thoroughly stymied the Bulls.

— Melissa Isaacson

Michael Jordan's missed break-away slam dunk in Game 3 stunned the Madison Square Garden crowd.

ED WAGNER

GAME 5
Bulls   96
Knicks   88
Bulls lead series, 3-2

Again the Bulls were bullied. Again they were forced to their very limit. And again Michael Jordan lowered his head and willed his team to victory.

Jordan's 15 of 17 on free throws — including 10 of 11 in the second half and 5 of 5 in the fourth quarter — is a good place to start. Jordan drove to the basket and drove hard in the fourth quarter, something he had not been able to do with regularity this series. He scored 13 of his 37 points in the fourth, almost exclusively on inside moves.

Jordan accounted for 13 of the Bulls' last 19 points and pulled them out of their deepest danger, when they led by only three with 1:25 remaining. Jordan canned a 16-footer and the free throw resulting from a foul called on Gerald Wilkins to boost the lead back to six with 36 seconds left.

The Knicks got no closer.

"Michael's Michael," Knicks coach Pat Riley said. "His game is to take it to the basket and challenge the defense. When you play against a guy like him, he tells you how much he wants to win by how hard he takes the ball to the basket."

GAME 6
Knicks   100
Bulls   86
Series tied, 3-3

No excuses. No complaints. The fouls were called, the opportunity was there, and the Bulls could do nothing but watch it go by.

Playing with chips the size of

ED WAGNER

Bulls coach Phil Jackson takes heat from New York fans after being ejected in the second half of Game 4 at Madison Square Garden.

Manhattan on their shoulders, the Knicks brought this series to its very brink, grabbing the fourth-quarter momentum with the same stubbornness they displayed throughout the series.

The loss was a mystery to the Bulls, who led by two points at the start of the fourth quarter only to watch their offense, their lead and any optimism disappear.

"We seemed to have control of the fourth quarter, and we have been great finishers all season," said Michael Jordan,

who paced a horrifyingly sluggish Bulls offense (39.8 percent shooting) with 21 points. "Then to finish it [the game] with no aggressiveness at all, that's really disappointing."

The Knicks, having lost any fear in facing the defending champions, brought the ball right at the Bulls. Patrick Ewing and John Starks finished with 27 points apiece. Xavier McDaniel had 24 points and 11 rebounds. Mark Jackson had 15 assists.

— Melissa Isaacson

GAME 7	
Bulls	**110**
Knicks	**81**
Bulls win series, 4-3	

The Bulls led by eight after one quarter, a positive sign in that the leader after the first period had been the victor in each of the previous six games. But there were hardly any sighs of relief.

Instead there was a sense of defiance by the Bulls, who often initiated the first contact and jumped into the Knicks' faces whenever it was necessary.

A double technical on Michael Jordan and Xavier McDaniel late in the first quarter followed a bit of jawing and some pushing between Scottie Pippen, McDaniel and Anthony Mason. If it meant no more than a changed attitude from the Bulls, that was enough.

It translated into loose balls retrieved and weak passes intercepted. The Bulls built their lead up to 11 in the second quarter, clung to a five-point lead at the half and blew it open in the third.

A run of 10-2 after halftime and 19-7 the remainder of the third quarter left the Bulls with a 15-point lead and the Knicks with an insurmountable hurdle.

"That third quarter took the heart out of them," said B.J. Armstrong.

Then, in the fourth quarter, the Bulls outscored the Knicks 18-6 in a killer span in which everything clicked.

When Patrick Ewing, who performed admirably, scoring 22 points with nine rebounds, drew his fifth foul with the Bulls up by 23, the "Hey-Hey, Goodbyes" began. By the time John Starks collected his sixth foul, with 33 seconds left, the taunting was mere revelry.

— Melissa Isaacson

A dejected John Starks (above) walks off the court after Game 7. Scottie Pippen (below) got physical when the series got down to the final game.

51

IN THE NICK OF TIME ...

There would be no backing down for the Bulls, who found their backs to the wall

Order was restored. Normalcy returned. Call off the therapy.

The Bulls found themselves just in the nick of time.

"They played like they are," said New York coach Pat Riley in a way only he, and perhaps Jean-Paul Sartre, could say it.

But it certainly was true enough.

The Bulls actually built a lead and held it, actually took the ball to the Knicks and came away without wounds, actually broke the 100-point barrier.

The defending champs absorbed every bit of energy from a Stadium crowd positively throbbing with emotion and knocked out the Knicks, 110-81, in the finale of the seven-game series to advance to the Eastern Conference finals.

"Never a Doubt" read the message on the giant scoreboard overhead as the final minutes ebbed in the last game of the best-of-seven. But who was anyone kidding?

This series was a hacking cough that wouldn't go away. A pain in the Bulls' neck. And back and shoulders and ankles ...

It took a reawakening to move on, to preserve the title that was at least partly responsible for this pressure-filled seven games to begin with.

By Melissa Isaacson

And the Bulls delivered.

There was Scottie Pippen with his second career triple-double, getting 17 points, 11 rebounds and 11 assists. There was Michael Jordan with 18 points in the first quarter, 29 in the half and 42 on the day. There was Horace Grant with a hard-earned 14 points, six rebounds, four blocked shots and four steals.

And there was a Bulls team that found the perfect blend of up-tempo offense and defensive abandon that had fueled them during the regular season, but had been only a memory against the Knicks.

There also was the 30 points off the bench and a 58 percent team shooting day. And, well, pretty much everything Bulls fans were expecting in this last headache-filled week and a half.

The Bulls were no longer 'sleepwalking' when Game 7 of the Eastern Conference semifinals tipped off. They rose to the occasion and played like the world champions they are.

"You've got to give New York credit," Jordan said. "They woke us up, if anything. We went through the series sleepwalking, we came out of this game with our backs to the wall and we responded. It seemed like the old Bulls that everyone expected."

The effort began from the opening minutes, when it was evident from the first offensive series that the Bulls were not about to back down.

"It was a tough enough series that we knew we had to bring out the best in us today," Pippen said. "It was a great feeling."

It had to be especially great for Pippen, who endured more than a week of criticism from the media and fans as he struggled to find his rhythm.

He was a different man for the final game, going to the bucket with his patented finger roll, draining his feathery jumper, plus hauling down rebounds to start the Bulls' break.

"We were upset about how we had been playing," Armstrong said, "and today we looked in the mirror and got back to playing Bulls basketball." •

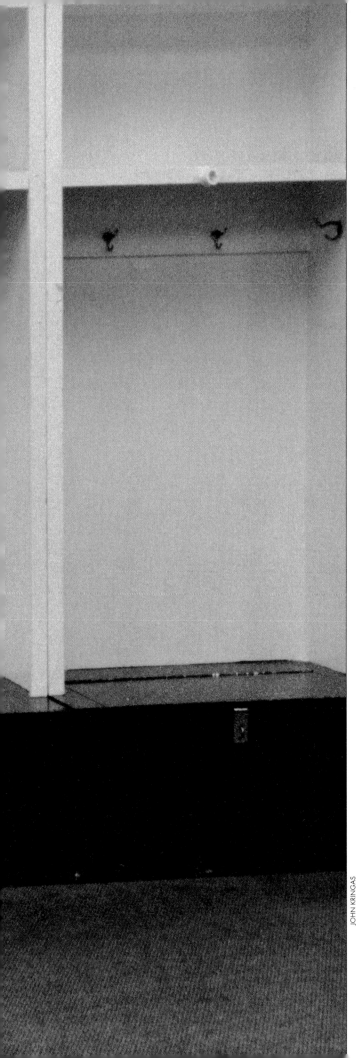

JOHN KRINGAS

STEPPING UP BIG-TIME

Bulls relieved at an honest ending to a distorted series with the Cavs

There was an image to protect, a reputation to uphold and, as if they could possibly forget, still a championship to defend.

So the whoops were controlled and comments careful when it was all over, but the relief on the Bulls' faces was palpable all the way from Richfield Coliseum to Michigan Avenue.

For the first time in a very long time, they had spared themselves unneeded aggravation. They had, in athletic parlance, stepped up. Big-time.

From Scottie Pippen and Horace Grant early, to Michael Jordan late, to Bill

By Melissa Isaacson

Cartwright in between, the Bulls gutted out a 99-94 victory in Game 6 of its series with the Cleveland Cavaliers to become Eastern Conference champions for the second consecutive year.

Next would come the Portland Trail Blazers and the NBA Finals. A formidable challenge. But for now, the Bulls savored this one night when everything fell into place.

"We're back in the Finals, which was one of our main goals," said Grant. "Now we just have to win it. No pressure at all, is there?"

Nothing they wouldn't be used to.

In the finale, with Jordan struggling mightily with

Cavs point guard Mark Price, who was severely weakened by a stomach virus, takes a break during the third quarter of Game 4 trying to settle his stomach.

55

Cavs center Brad Daugherty tries some "in your face" defense against Michael Jordan in Game 3 of the Eastern Conference finals.

his shooting, having hit just 5 of 20 from the field through three quarters, they simply stared it down.

Pippen, a man who fought off injuries, self-doubt and the unrelenting scrutiny of a demanding public during these playoffs, held the Bulls together, finishing with 29 points, 12 rebounds, five assists, four steals and four blocked shots.

"I just can't say enough about Pippen coming out and really leading us and giving us the edge and energy we needed to get the ball upcourt and get us aggressive offensively," said coach Phil Jackson.

Grant, likewise, would assume heavy responsibility and come through it with 20 points, nine rebounds and two blocked shots. And Cartwright would gut out 41 minutes and finish with 10 points and nine rebounds.

They would carry the Bulls as long and as far as they could and then, gladly, they would relin-quish the fourth-quarter heroics to the man they had seen perform them so many times before.

"This is what the supporting cast is all about," said Grant. "It's what teammates are all about."

"It was a relief to get this over," said John Paxson, who gave the Bulls their first tie of the final period with an 18-foot jumper. "Early in the fourth, it was beginning to look like we were going to pull that old number from Game 6 in New York."

But in the end, the Bulls, their defense and their savior, went for the kill.

So this series wound up the way you figured it would start, the way it seemed destined to play out.

Good basketball, close basketball. Dramatic ending. An honest ending, it turned out, to a distorted five games preceding it.

"It was a great game between two divisional opponents who have met each other so many times over the years," Jackson said. "A fitting ending right down to the wire, a classic game."

Who, Cavs coach Lenny Wilkens was asked, would he pick in the finals? "I'm not picking anybody in the finals," Wilkens said. "I'm just going to sit back and enjoy it."

For the Bulls, there is enjoyment yet.

"This is no time to celebrate when you're going to the dance," said Cartwright. "You celebrate after the dance." ●

GAME 1

Bulls	103
Cavaliers	89

Bulls lead series, 1-0

Hey, Chicago. Basketball is back. The real McCoy. Fast breaks and screen-and-rolls. Bloodless defense and free-throw shooting and everything.

The Bulls were so happy, they jumped right in and wallowed around in it, roaming the Stadium court with joyful abandon and securing Game 1 of the Eastern Conference finals with ease over the Cleveland Cavaliers.

After grinding out a grueling — not to mention bruising — seven days of gritty basketball, New York style, this indeed looked like a different sport.

The Bulls hit 15 of their first 20 shots, opened up a 20-point lead before half-time and withstood the Cavs' greatest punch — one that trimmed the lead to seven early in the fourth — to close out the victory with no serious threat.

"We felt the first game in the series is the hardest one," Michael Jordan said. "We have to defend the home court, as we learned in the New York series."

GAME 2

Cavaliers	107
Bulls	81

Series tied, 1-1

This game at the Stadium was not merely bad. It was shockingly bad. Embarrassingly bad. Near record-setting bad.

"I've never sat through an exhibition of basketball like that in my life," said Bulls coach Phil Jackson. "This team

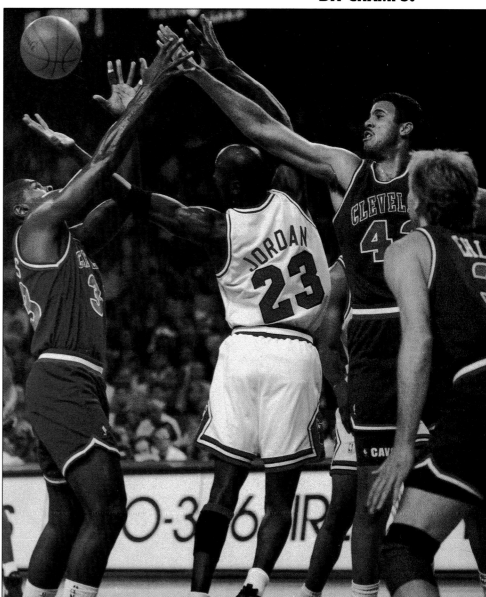

ED WAGNER

Jordan and the Bulls got more than they could handle from the Cavaliers in Game 2, an embarrassingly bad blowout at the Stadium.

deserved to be booed off the floor."

They might have been if anybody had waited around until the end. The loss was the Bulls' worst at home since 1985.

It could have been called a comedy of errors except that no one but the 15 or so guys on the Cavaliers bench was laughing.

The Bulls missed their first 13 shots of the game. They hit just 3 of 21 from the field in the first quarter for 14 percent to

fall behind 30-14 after one, and trailed 59-33 at the half. Talk about digging holes.

The Cavs, questioned for their effort in Game 1, came out determined, to say the least.

"We were pretty confident we'd come out a lot more intense than Game 1 and be more active," Cleveland coach Lenny Wilkens said. "I thought we did that."

- Melissa Isaacson

Michael Jordan tries to restrain Scott Williams, who argues a foul call in the fourth quarter of Game 3.

GAME 3
Bulls   **105**
Cavaliers   **96**
Bulls lead series, 2-1

OK, let's get this straight. Anger is good, embarrassment better. Forget shooting and rebounding and all those other trivial details.

As the Bulls wind their way through this treacherous journey they call the NBA playoffs, motivation is where it all turns.

And with their road victory over Cleveland in Game 3, the Bulls took the lead in this latest psychological endeavor.

In an eerie switch that coach Phil Jackson called "a reversal of fortune," the Bulls took the Cavs out early, surging to a 26-4 bulge late in the first quarter, and rode that cushion to the end without relinquishing the lead.

One of the main factors was Michael Jordan attaching himself to Cleveland point guard Mark Price — not his usual assignment — to completely disrupt the Cavaliers' offense.

"That was of his own volition," Jackson said. "We were mismatched on our presses after free throws a couple of times, and he liked it and wanted to stay with it."

GAME 4
Cavaliers   **99**
Bulls   **85**
Series tied, 2-2

Analysis was scarce in the Bulls' locker room, as elusive as a fourth-quarter hero, a Scottie Pippen shot, a break of any kind.

This one hurt. Like the Halley's comet of a three-pointer by Mike Sanders, which squelched the Bulls' spirit and their comeback, this loss to Cleveland hit them hard.

The best-of-seven Eastern Conference finals was now tied at two games apiece and headed back to Chicago.

Home-court advantage was still intact. But reality told the Bulls they could have avoided a trip back to Cleveland for a now-necessary Game 6.

The Cavs' attack, if not altogether sharp, was balanced and full of step-up performances, with five players scoring 13 points or better.

The Bulls' attack was not.

Scottie Pippen inexplicably took only three second-half shots, missing all of them. Michael Jordan may have been distracted by the incessant booing that began after Danny Ferry punched him and was ejected in the second quarter, and continued until Jordan boarded the bus.

"It looks like this [series] is going to go the length," said coach Phil Jackson, resignedly.

— Melissa Isaacson

58

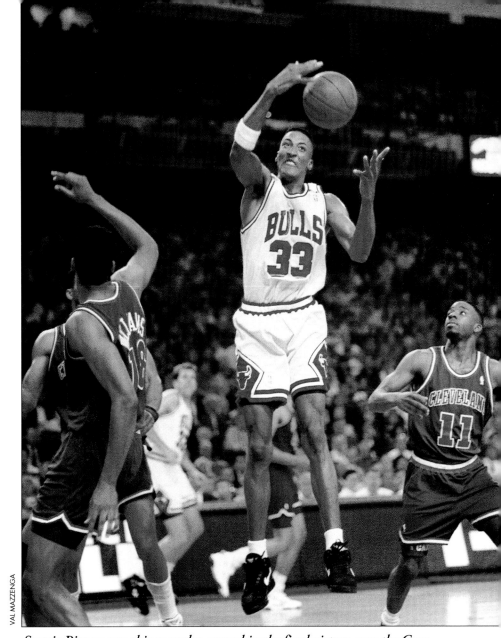

Scottie Pippen gets things under control in the final victory over the Cavs.

GAME 5

Bulls	112
Cavaliers	89

Bulls lead series, 3-2

It was much more than a catharsis. A blood-letting was more like it, as the Bulls' Doberman mentality returned to the Stadium with a force that only their longing fans could fully appreciate.

The Bulls walloped Cleveland, enveloping the Cavs with an astounding 39-18 fourth-quarter edge that made a close game through three quarters seem a mirage.

Scott Williams finished with 12 points and seven rebounds and Cliff Levingston with 12 points as the Bulls virtually shut down the Cavs' front line of Brad Daugherty (slowed by a jammed finger on his shooting hand), Larry Nance, Mike Sanders and John "Hot Rod" Williams to a combined 33 points.

Nearly everything went right for the Bulls in their amazing final period. Clinging to a two-point lead at the end of three quarters, the Bulls took command early in the period, starting the fourth with a 15-0 run to coast into Game 6 in Cleveland needing one victory to advance to the NBA Finals.

GAME 6

Bulls	99
Cavaliers	94

Bulls win series, 4-2

It was right where they wanted to be, where they had to be, Michael Jordan said. At a place and time where they could "taste it and smell it."

Jordan scored 16 of his 29 points in the final quarter, helped the Bulls rally from a seven-point deficit early in the period and pushed them past ties at 87 with 3:19 remaining and at 93 with 48 seconds left.

The Cavs would manage just one more point, a free throw by Mark Price, and the Bulls would close it out with free throws by Jordan and Scottie Pippen.

"I was fighting myself for the first three quarters because I wanted to win so badly," Jordan said. "I didn't want to think about going back to Chicago [for Game 7]. Somehow I found my confidence in the fourth quarter to the point where I could lead this team to victory."

The game was tied at the end of three, and even after the Bulls climbed back to lead 93-90, there was Price canning a three-pointer to give the Cavs hope again.

"The last thing I wanted to see was Price coming down and hitting that three-pointer," Bulls coach Phil Jackson said. "It just shows the kind of effort Cleveland had in this series, and the heart they have."

— Melissa Isaacson

VAL MAZZENGA

59

OVERTIME

Back to the Finals: 'What a long, strange trip it has been'

The details – and what incredible details they were – are secondary. Mere blips in one huge, amazing evening. The heart-pounding fourth quarter. The courageous bench contribution. The records that fell as the Chicago Bulls made history.

All of them will fade with time. And what we will be left with, days from now, months from now, years from now, is the big picture. The memory of watching a team achieve pure, unadulterated satisfaction.

This was victory just as sweet as it gets. Their 97-93 triumph over the Portland Trail Blazers in Game 6 gave the Bulls the 1992 NBA championship, their second consecutive world title and an occasion that had something for everyone.

"John Paxson turned to me in the locker room and said, 'What

Michael Jordan, MVP of the NBA Finals for the second consecutive year, leads the victory celebration.

a long, strange trip it has been,' " Chicago coach Phil Jackson said. "And he wasn't just quoting the Grateful Dead. It has been a long, strange trip. Last year was the honeymoon. This year was an odyssey."

The night was for everyone who has ever wanted to give up.

By Melissa Isaacson

Everyone who was ever tired of their job or sick of their boss. Everyone who ever questioned whether the goal was worth the aggravation, whether the destination was worth the journey.

This was about Bobby Hansen, a nine-year veteran who wanted only to belong, to contribute. Who rarely played until this Finals series, then calmly entered the game in the fourth quarter, hit a three-pointer, made a steal and jump-started this team to its destiny.

It was about Stacey King, the most beleaguered of third-year players who grew up and decided it was best to keep his dissatisfaction private. Who grabbed hold

of the only significant playing time he has had since early in the season and helped sustain this team when it needed it most.

It was about Scott Williams and his eight rebounds and two blocked shots, and B.J. Armstrong with his four assists and key jumper to pull the Bulls to within five with 9 minutes 10 seconds left. It was about Cliff Levingston drawing fouls and, as always, urging on his teammates.

It was about a team defense that held the Trail Blazers to a record-low 14 fourth-quarter points, enabling the Bulls to come back from a 17-point, late-third-quarter deficit. About an offense that would not quit. And a crowd that would not let them.

Paxson said, "Going into the fourth quarter, Phil said, 'Fifteen points is nothing if we can regain momentum,' and it worked just like he said."

This was all about Bill Cartwright and his underrated defense and unbreakable will. About Paxson with his veteran

61

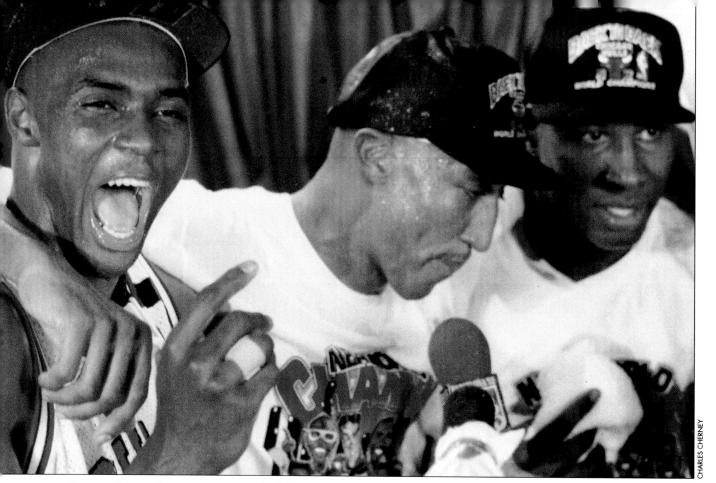

Horace Grant, Scottie Pippen and Cliff Levingston celebrate their second NBA title in front of the media.

smarts, his in-your-face job on Terry Porter and his clutch-as-can-be six-of-nine shooting for 13 points. About Horace Grant, muscling inside, about brushing himself off time and time again, about five rebounds and a block of a Buck Williams shot they will be reliving in the highlight films.

It was about Scottie Pippen crushing the demons and muting the critics and leading the fourth-quarter band of renegades with poise and cool. It was about letting his skills rise to the occasion and finishing this unforgettable night with 26 points, five rebounds and four assists.

And finally, it was about Michael Jordan, the man who defies explanation, who capped this season with 12 of the Bulls'

last 17 points to finish with 33 for the night, and who led the Bulls in scoring in every game of the 1992 postseason.

Jordan was the Most Valuable Player of the NBA Finals, a unanimous selection, an undeniable selection and a repeat selection.

"I'm just so glad Chicago drafted me eight years ago," Jordan said. "If they didn't, I don't think I could do what I did, being a part of back-to-back championships. This is a great town to play for. I love it. And I hope to play here forever."

This was a pulsating Chicago Stadium that engulfed the Bulls with emotion.

It was the team gathering in the catacombs of the old barn, and in the middle of all the crazi-

ness, looking up at their coach.

"Great job, fellas," Jackson whispered to them, and as one they nodded back.

It was the last Lord's Prayer of the season, recited in unison, and a champagne shower to punctuate the blessing.

It was June Jackson grasping her husband's face and embracing his soaked body. And it was about her husband hugging their five children, one by one.

It was Pippen standing in his still blood-soaked uniform with a smile that could have swallowed up the locker room.

And it was big Horace grabbing Horace Jr. and hanging on.

"How sweet it is," said Jackson.

"It puts everything right where

it should be," said Cartwright. "We couldn't possibly have imagined a better ending."

"The struggle," said Grant, "makes it that much sweeter. When the last seconds ticked off the clock, all the excitement and joy of the season shot straight through my body."

"I hope," said Paxson, "that the people of Chicago appreciate what we've done. There's only one way to achieve something once you've won and that's to win again. This is truly special."

Then, as quickly as they had arrived, they were beckoned away.

"Grab that trophy and let's show it to them," Jackson cried out as he led the march back to courtside.

"You got it," shouted Jordan. "Let's go."

And suddenly, they were back where it all began – under the stark white banner that greeted them in this season's opening game.

"Two of them," cried Jordan as he circled the court, glimmering trophy held aloft.

There was Will Perdue and Cartwright embracing, and Paxson and his father sharing a remarkably quiet moment.

And then there were all of them. Together. Doing a giant line dance on top of the scorer's table. Linking arms and singing and toasting the crowd. Milking it all and soaking it up. Every last bit of it. ●

Michael Jordan's remarkable opening game performance – a record 35 points in the first half – set the tone for the Finals.

CHARLES CHERNEY

AIRING IT OUT

Jordan's three-point barrage in Game 1 makes Finals history

CHARLES CHERNEY

Bill Cartwright (right) and the rest of the Bulls huddle outside the locker room before the opening game of the NBA Finals.

Long after his teammates had hit the road following the morning practice, Michael Jordan killed some time by hanging around the team's practice facility in the Chicago suburb of Deerfield.

Alone on a court with just a basketball and an agenda, Jordan collected his thoughts during a rare moment of playoff privacy and practiced shooting three-pointers with no one around to bother him.

Shoot and go shag it. Shoot and shag. Over and over, Jordan shot threes until his timing was as perfect as a Swiss watch.

No one knew, not even Jordan himself, that he would soon spend Game 1 in the very same mode – shooting threes with no one in his face. Only this time, he didn't have to shag.

"The only way you can stop Michael," said Portland's Cliff Robinson afterwards, "is to take him off the court."

The Trail Blazers did manage to stop Jordan for those 14 minutes when he was off the court.

Otherwise, no dice.

Jordan hit his first three-pointer with six minutes gone in the first period, and then canned five more in the next 17 minutes.

And that wasn't all.

As Jordan revealed on a cable TV cooking show last fall, one of his favorite creations is a huge pot of gumbo. So Jordan created his own kind of "hoops gumbo" in the first half, adding a few jams and fallaway jumpers to his bevy of threes, making the Blazers stew for the rest of the evening.

In all, Jordan scored 35 points in the half, an NBA Finals record.

"The guy had an incredible scoring spree," said Portland's Clyde Drexler. "There's nothing you can do about it. That's where we wanted him to shoot."

Drexler was so confident that Jordan's spree was just a freakish thing that he just about dared Jordan to try and do it again.

"I'm gonna give him those same shots in Game 2," Drexler said.

"I believe it," Jordan said when told of Drexler's remark. "I surprised everybody. But I'm not going to go out with the plan of shooting six or seven threes. I'm gonna feel him out."

In etching his name into the NBA record books again, Jordan tied Bill Laimbeer and Michael Cooper for most three-pointers in an NBA Finals game. It is very likely that's the only thing in life that Jordan shares with Laimbeer.

When he was informed that Detroit Pistons center Laimbeer was one of the players whose record he had just tied, a pained look crossed Jordan's face.

"If you would've told me that," he said, "I'd have shot more."

– **Paul Sullivan**

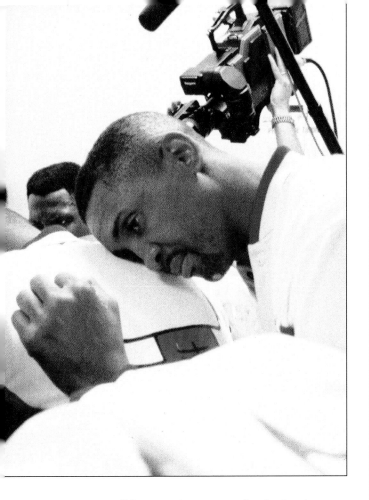

GAME 1

Bulls	122
Trail Blazers	89

Bulls lead series, 1-0

Portland (89)	Min	FG-A	FT-A	Reb O-T	A	PF	Pts
Jerome Kersey	27	3-8	1-1	1-7	3	3	7
Buck Williams	18	1-1	1-2	1-2	0	4	3
Kevin Duckworth	25	3-5	1-1	1-5	2	3	7
Clyde Drexler	31	5-14	6-7	4-5	7	4	16
Terry Porter	32	5-9	3-4	1-6	2	2	13
Cliff Robinson	24	7-14	2-2	0-2	0	5	16
Mark Bryant	21	5-8	0-0	3-5	0	1	10
Danny Ainge	22	3-8	1-2	0-0	1	1	8
Ennis Whatley	13	2-5	0-0	0-1	0	1	4
John Pack	13	1-5	2-2	0-1	1	1	4
Wayne Cooper	8	0-0	0-0	0-2	0	1	0
Alaa Abdelnaby	6	0-1	1-2	0-2	0	0	1
Totals	**240**	**35-78**	**18-23**	**38**	**16**	**26**	**89**

Percentages: FG .449, FT .783. **Three-point goals:** 1-6, .167 (Ainge 1-2, Drexler 0-2, Porter 0-2). **Team rebounds:** 5. **Blocked shots:** 4 (Cooper 2, Duckworth, Ainge). **Turnovers:** 21 (Kersey 5, B.Williams 4, Drexler 4, Duckworth 2, Bryant 2, Porter, Ainge, Pack, Abdelnaby). **Steals:** 7 (Drexler 2, Whatley 2, B.Williams, Ainge, Pack). **Illegal defense:** 1.

Chicago (122)	Min	FG-A	FT-A	Reb O-T	A	PF	Pts
Scottie Pippen	33	8-14	8-9	3-9	10	2	24
Horace Grant	31	5-8	1-2	3-7	2	0	11
Bill Cartwright	16	1-4	3-4	3-5	0	3	5
John Paxson	19	2-4	0-0	0-0	5	4	4
Michael Jordan	34	16-27	1-1	2-3	11	0	39
Scott Williams	28	6-6	0-0	4-9	1	4	12
B.J. Armstrong	29	5-11	0-0	0-3	6	3	11
Bobby Hansen	14	2-4	1-2	0-1	2	1	5
Cliff Levingston	15	4-7	0-0	0-3	1	1	8
Stacey King	15	0-3	1-2	1-2	0	2	1
Will Perdue	6	1-3	0-2	0-2	0	1	2
Totals	**240**	**50-91**	**15-22**	**44**	**38**	**21**	**122**

Percentages: FG .549, FT .682. **Three-point goals:** 7-15, .467 (Jordan 6-10, Armstrong 1-1, Pippen 0-1, Paxson 0-1, Hansen 0-1, Levingston 0-1). **Team rebounds:** 9. **Blocked shots:** 7 (Grant 3, S.Williams 2, Pippen, King). **Turnovers:** 11 (Armstrong 3, Cartwright 2, S.Williams 2, Pippen, Jordan, Levingston, King). **Steals:** 7 (Pippen 2, Jordan 2, Grant, Paxson, King). **Illegal defense:** 1.

Portland	30	21	17	21	—	89
Chicago	33	33	38	18	—	122

A: 18,676.

Count yourself fortunate if you witnessed Michael Jordan's magic moment in any form at all.

"I was in a zone," Jordan said of his 35-point first half, which included a record-setting six three-pointers. "My threes felt like free throws. I didn't know what I was doing, but they were going in."

But the most encouraging thing for the Bulls was that beyond the bionic performance of Jordan there was a team effort that rekindled memories of the defending champs at their very best.

Scottie Pippen scored 24 points and just missed a triple-double. All 12 Bulls scored as they went up 66-51 at the half, 104-68 after three.

The Blazers were razor-sharp early, nailing their first seven shots while the Bulls struggled. It still looked like a real game at that point.

The teams went back and forth for the first part of the second quarter until Jordan took the game, his game, into a different realm.

When the fireworks subsided, the Bulls had taken a 66-49 lead. Perhaps the scariest thing for the Blazers was that they were shooting well. Sixty percent in the first half to 53 percent for the Bulls.

But Portland committed 12 turnovers leading to 23 Bulls points in the half, and that told the story as much as anything.

— Melissa Isaacson

GAME 2 (OT)

Trail Blazers		**115**
Bulls		**104**

Series tied, 1-1

Portland (115)	Min	FG-A	FT-A	Reb O-T	A	PF	Pts
Jerome Kersey	41	6-11	0-0	4-8	4	6	12
Buck Williams	48	7-9	5-5	3-14	2	2	19
Kevin Duckworth	43	6-15	2-2	0-8	4	3	14
Clyde Drexler	38	8-20	10-10	2-7	8	6	26
Terry Porter	49	8-17	7-9	0-1	3	1	24
Cliff Robinson	18	0-2	3-8	0-2	2	4	3
Danny Ainge	23	7-10	3-4	1-2	4	4	17
Ennis Whatley	5	0-0	0-0	0-0	0	0	0
Totals	**265**	**42-84**	**30-38**	**42**	**27**	**26**	**115**

Percentages: FG .500, FT .789. **Three-point goals:** 1-12, .083 (Porter 1-5, Ainge 0–3, Drexler 0-4). **Team rebounds:** 12. **Blocked shots:** 3 (B.Williams, Duckworth, Porter). **Turnovers:** 9 (B.Williams 3, Porter 3, Duckworth 2, Kersey). **Steals:** 7 (Kersey 2, Drexler 2, B.Williams, Duckworth, Porter). **Illegal defense:** 1.

Chicago (104)	Min	FG-A	FT-A	Reb O-T	A	PF	Pts
Scottie Pippen	48	6-19	4-6	3-8	10	4	16
Horace Grant	46	4-6	2-3	2-12	7	4	10
Bill Cartwright	34	4-4	2-4	1-4	1	3	10
John Paxson	42	6-14	0-0	0-1	4	2	16
Michael Jordan	50	16-32	7-9	1-5	10	5	39
Scott Williams	20	1-3	1-2	1-9	0	2	3
Cliff Levingston	9	3-6	1-2	1-1	1	2	7
B.J. Armstrong	7	0-1	0-0	0-0	1	2	0
Will Perdue	3	0-0	0-0	1-1	0	2	0
Bobby Hansen	6	1-1	0-0	0-0	0	3	3
Totals	**265**	**41-86**	**17-26**	**41**	**34**	**29**	**104**

Percentages: FG .477, FT .654. **Three-point goals:** 5-15, .333 (Paxson 4-7, Hansen 1-1, Pippen 0-3, Jordan 0-4). **Team rebounds:** 9. **Blocked shots:** 7 (Grant 5, Cartwright, S.Williams). **Turnovers:** 15 (Pippen 6, Jordan 5, Cartwright, Paxson, S.Williams, Hansen). **Steals:** 5 (Pippen 3, Grant, Jordan). **Technical fouls:** Jordan, 4:25 fourth.

Portland	31	23	16	27	18	—	115
Chicago	23	22	32	20	7	—	104

A: 18,676.

Danny Ainge proved to be the hero in Game 2, scoring 9 points in overtime to lift the Blazers.

JIM PRISCHING

"Momentum," said Portland hero Danny Ainge, "is a fickle thing." And his nine-point overtime period showed his philosophy was right on.

With a vicious swiftness, the Blazers rallied at their lowest point: down 10 and without their leader, Clyde Drexler, who had fouled out with 4:36 remaining after scoring 26 points.

Forcing the game into overtime with a 15-5 run the remainder of the fourth quarter, the Blazers carried forward their momentum into the extra period, in which they outscored the defending NBA champions 18-7.

"It was a gift in our hands, and we just gave it away," said a dejected Horace Grant.

Michael Jordan put the Bulls ahead by two with a double-clutching bucket down low with 31 seconds showing. But after Kevin Duckworth tied it again with an open eight-foot jumper with 13 seconds left, Jordan's 16-foot jumper hit the back of the rim at the buzzer.

The Blazers delivered the lethal blow in less than 30 seconds — with a Terry Porter three-pointer and a quick transition layup from Ainge — to give Portland a 110-102 lead with 1:03 left in overtime.

"Momentum is an ever-changing thing in a playoff series," Ainge reminded.

An ever-annoying thing as well.

— Melissa Isaacson

Clyde Drexler scored 26 points before fouling out – leaving it up to his Portland teammates to overcome a 10-point deficit.

JIM PRISCHING

JOHN KRINGAS

GAME 3

Bulls	94
Trail Blazers	84

Bulls lead series, 2-1

Chicago (94)	Min	FG-A	FT-A	Reb O-T	A	PF	Pts
Scottie Pippen	43	6-15	6-8	1-8	7	4	18
Horace Grant	37	7-12	4-5	1-8	6	4	18
Bill Cartwright	25	3-7	0-2	2-7	3	6	6
John Paxson	32	3-5	2-2	0-0	2	1	8
Michael Jordan	41	11-22	4-4	2-7	4	4	26
Scott Williams	19	1-5	0-0	1-6	2	4	2
B.J. Armstrong	17	2-5	0-2	0-0	1	1	4
Bobby Hansen	10	1-3	0-0	0-0	0	0	3
Cliff Levingston	7	0-0	1-2	0-2	0	1	1
Stacey King	9	3-4	2-4	2-4	0	1	8
Totals	**240**	**37-78**	**19-29**	**42**	**25**	**26**	**94**

Percentages: FG .474, FT .750. **Three-point goals:** 1-4, .250 (Hansen 1-1, Pippen 0-1, Paxson 0-1, Jordan 0-1).
Team rebounds: 13. **Technical fouls:** Chicago coach Phil Jackson.

Portland (84)	Min	FG-A	FT-A	Reb O-T	A	PF	Pts
Jerome Kersey	36	4-13	3-6	6-12	1	4	11
Buck Williams	41	1-5	4-4	1-9	2	5	6
Kevin Duckworth	25	5-11	1-2	2-4	0	6	11
Clyde Drexler	42	9-17	12-12	1-9	3	4	32
Terry Porter	44	3-7	1-2	1-5	4	2	7
Cliff Robinson	25	2-11	1-2	1-3	1	3	5
Danny Ainge	23	4-12	3-4	1-1	1	2	12
Ennis Whatley	4	0-2	0-0	0-0	0	0	0
Totals	**240**	**28-78**	**25-32**	**43**	**12**	**26**	**84**

Percentages: FG .308, FT .500. **Three-point goals:** 3-11, .273 (Drexler 2-4, Ainge 1-5, Porter 0-1, Robinson 0-1).
Team rebounds: 10. **Technical fouls:** None.

Chicago	34	20	16	24	— 94
Portland	26	19	15	24	— 84

A: 12,888.

68

Portland coach Rick Adelman (left) shows his displeasure as his team self-destructs against the Bulls in Game 3.

If this were a game of semantics and a series of expectations, then this Bulls victory could be fairly assessed as unattractive.

However, that hardly mattered to the Bulls. They did what champions do, and they did it with an oppressive defense and a balanced offense and a recently acquired knowledge of what happens when you stop playing before the buzzer sounds.

"For the most part," summed up Michael Jordan, "it was beautiful enough to win."

Three Bulls — Jordan, Scottie Pippen and Horace Grant — were in double figures by halftime, and they finished with 26, 18 and 18 points respectively.

Both Pippen and Grant had eight rebounds, and Pippen also had two blocked shots to one for Grant. The Bulls bench, led by Scott Williams' six rebounds and Stacey King's eight points and four rebounds in relief of Bill Cartwright, was solid.

The Bulls shot 47 percent while caging the lethargic Blazers in a half-court game, and holding them to a dismal 36 percent shooting from the floor. Only Clyde Drexler, with a game-high 32 points on 53 percent shooting from the field, provided any consistency.

"They controlled the tempo, we shot poorly and never got in the groove," Portland coach Rick Adelman said. "We were totally out of sync."

— Melissa Isaacson

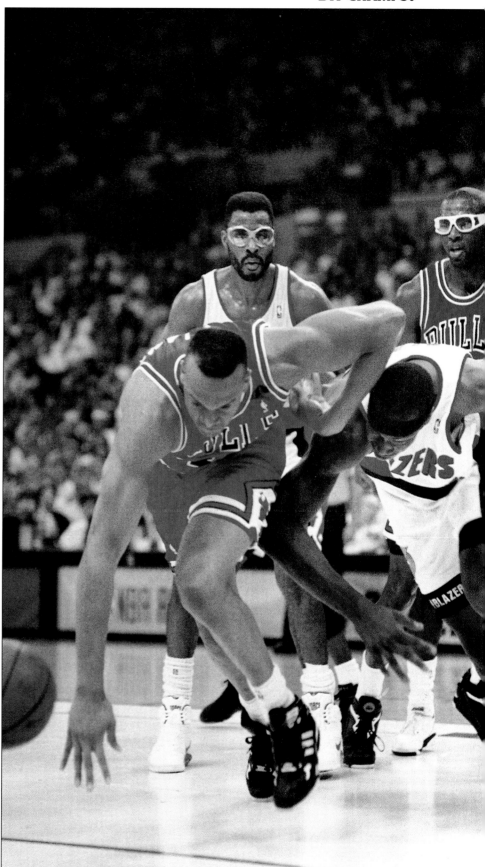

JOHN KRINGAS

69

JOHN KRINGAS

Buck Williams loses the handle, but the host Blazers were able to hang on to a slim victory in Game 4.

GAME 4

| Trail Blazers | **93** |
| Bulls | **88** |

Series tied, 2-2

Chicago (88)	Min	FG-A	FT-A	Reb O-T	A	PF	Pts
Scottie Pippen	32	8-13	1-4	3-9	6	4	17
Horace Grant	44	4-10	0-0	1-10	1	4	8
Bill Cartwright	38	4-8	1-2	0-4	2	3	9
John Paxson	30	3-7	1-2	0-0	0	4	9
Michael Jordan	44	11-26	8-8	0-5	6	4	32
B.J. Armstrong	18	3-7	0-1	1-1	2	2	6
Scott Williams	14	1-1	3-3	0-1	0	4	5
Cliff Levingston	15	0-4	0-0	2-3	1	1	0
Craig Hodges	5	1-1	0-0	0-0	0	1	2
Totals	**240**	**35-77**	**14-20**	**33**	**18**	**27**	**88**

Percentages: FG .455, FT .700. **Three-point goals:** 4-12, .333 (Paxson 2-4, Jordan 2-6, Armstrong 0-1, Grant 0-1). **Team rebounds:** 11. **Blocked shots:** 1 (S.Williams). **Turnovers:** 16 (Jordan 5, Pippen 3, Cartwright 2, Hodges 2, Grant, Paxson, Armstrong, S.Williams). **Steals:** 7 (Cartwright 2, Pippen, Grant, Paxson, Armstrong, Hodges). **Illegal defense:** 1.

Portland (93)	Min	FG-A	FT-A	Reb O-T	A	PF	Pts
Jerome Kersey	43	8-12	5-6	1-4	5	3	21
Buck Williams	32	3-7	0-0	3-4	0	3	6
Kevin Duckworth	26	3-11	1-1	3-11	2	3	7
Clyde Drexler	43	9-22	3-6	3-8	9	2	21
Terry Porter	45	5-10	3-4	1-6	4	0	14
Cliff Robinson	27	6-11	5-10	2-6	4	4	17
Danny Ainge	21	3-8	0-0	2-6	3	4	7
Ennis Whatley	3	0-0	0-0	0-0	1	0	0
Totals	**240**	**37-81**	**17-27**	**45**	**28**	**19**	**93**

Percentages: FG .457, FT .630. **Three-point goals:** 2-9, .222 (Ainge 1-2, Porter 1-3, Drexler 0-4). **Team rebounds:** 13. **Blocked shots:** 6 (Drexler 3, B.Williams, Duckworth, Robinson). **Turnovers:** 13 (B.Williams 3, Kersey 2, Drexler 2, Porter 2, Ainge 2, Duckworth, Robinson). **Steals:** 11 (Kersey 2, Drexler 2, Robinson 2, Ainge 2, B.Williams, Porter, Whatley). **Flagrant foul:** Kersey, 7:43 4th.

Chicago	26	22	21	19	—	88
Portland	18	27	21	27	—	93

A: 12,888.

You looked at the scoreboard and wondered how the Trail Blazers were still in the game. Wondered how, with poor shot selection and poor shooting and still more cerebral letdowns to add to their reputation, they could actually put together a potent enough rally to take the lead.

But when they continued to push, scraping together enough free throws and forcing enough turnovers to win, you stopped wondering.

Utilizing a smothering defense and getting their offensive act together, the Blazers won in Bulls fashion, overtaking the defending champions with a late surge.

"They took this game, no doubt about it," said Bulls reserve Cliff Levingston. "They wanted the win, and they seized the opportunity."

The Blazers sure took their sweet time getting started, but then outscored the Bulls 19-8 in the final 7:47. Portland took its first lead of the game at 83-82 with 3:35 left as Clyde Drexler, after stripping the ball from Michael Jordan on a drive, muscled one in off an assist from Terry Porter.

The Blazers sank six of eight free throws down the stretch and delivered the fatal blow just as it looked like the Bulls might pull out the victory after all.

A drive by John Paxson brought the Bulls to within three at 91-88 with 33 seconds left. But just as quick, Porter was breaking downcourt for an easy layup and the final margin of victory.

— **Melissa Isaacson**

Portland's Williams was up to the challenge in Game 4, denying a shot by Michael Jordan.

70

The Bulls edged closer to their second consecutive title behind Jordan's 46-point performance in Game 5.

Until now, the Bulls may have been mad, but it was the Trail Blazers who had gotten even.

But the defending world champions took one step closer to preserving their title as Michael Jordan led the way with 46 points despite an ankle injury. Scottie Pippen came on strong with 24 points, 11 rebounds and nine assists as the Bulls moved one victory away from another NBA title.

Trying desperately to avoid another late letdown, the Bulls never let the Trail Blazers closer than nine points in the fourth quarter as the bench came through.

Scott Williams, Cliff Levingston, Stacey King and Bobby Hansen all helped preserve control.

With six Bulls and five Blazers carrying four fouls or more in the fourth quarter, including five for Jordan and Horace Grant, this game was a tightrope walk in the latter stages.

And in the end, the Trail Blazers fell off. Clyde Drexler fouled out on a charge into Pippen with 2:42 remaining. It was a non-shooting foul, but Jordan hit two free throws on a subsequent foul by Jerome Kersey at the 1:58 mark to push the Bulls' lead to 114-101.

Jordan's 46 marked an all-time playoff high against a Portland defense. Drexler led Portland with 30 points and 10 rebounds.

– Melissa Isaacson

GAME 5

Bulls	119
Trailblazers	106

Bulls lead series, 3-2

Chicago (119)	Min	FG-A	FT-A	Reb O-T	A	PF	Pts
Scottie Pippen	45	8-15	8-9	3-11	9	4	24
Horace Grant	33	2-4	2-5	0-5	3	6	6
Bill Cartwright	19	2-4	0-0	1-3	3	4	4
John Paxson	33	6-11	0-0	0-1	3	2	12
Michael Jordan	42	14-23	16-19	0-5	4	5	46
Scott Williams	23	2-4	3-4	3-4	3	5	7
B.J. Armstrong	17	2-4	4-4	0-0	0	1	8
Cliff Levingston	13	2-3	2-2	2-3	1	1	6
Stacey King	8	1-4	2-2	0-1	0	4	4
Bobby Hansen	5	1-1	0-0	1-1	0	1	2
Craig Hodges	1	0-0	0-0	0-0	0	0	0
Will Perdue	1	0-0	0-0	0-0	0	0	0
Totals	**240**	**40-73**	**37-45**	**34**	**26**	**33**	**119**

Percentages: FG .548, FT .822. **Three-point goals:** 2-6, .333 (Jordan 2-4, Paxson 0-1, Pippen 0-1).
Team rebounds: 8. **Blocked shots:** 6 (Grant 4, Jordan, Levingston). **Turnovers:** 14 (Jordan 4, Pippen 3, Grant 3, Cartwright 2, Paxson, Armstrong). **Steals:** 6 (Pippen 2, Paxson 2, Grant, Cartwright).

Portland (106)	Min	FG-A	FT-A	Reb O-T	A	PF	Pts
Jerome Kersey	36	7-17	0-0	8-12	3	5	14
Buck Williams	31	3-6	0-0	3-7	0	3	6
Kevin Duckworth	28	3-6	7-11	2-7	0	5	13
Clyde Drexler	41	9-21	12-14	5-10	3	6	30
Terry Porter	46	5-12	7-8	1-2	8	3	17
Danny Ainge	28	5-13	3-4	0-3	3	5	14
Cliff Robinson	26	3-4	5-5	1-4	4	6	11
Ennis Whatley	1	0-0	0-0	0-0	0	0	0
Robert Pack	3	0-1	1-2	0-0	0	1	1
Totals	**240**	**35-80**	**35-44**	**45**	**21**	**34**	**106**

Percentages: FG .438, FT .795. **Three-point goals:** 1-7, .143 (Ainge 1-4, Drexler 0-3). **Team rebounds:** 8.
Blocked shots: 3 (B.Williams, Drexler, Porter).
Turnovers: 18 (Kersey 6, Drexler 4, Duckworth 3, Porter 3, B.Williams, Ainge). **Steals:** 5 (Porter 3, Kersey 2). **Technical fouls:** B.Williams, 9:49 first. **Illegal defense:** 1.

Chicago	39	27	28	25	—	119
Portland	26	28	24	28	—	106

A: 12,888.

Clyde Drexler's 30-point performance wasn't enough to spark Portland, which never got closer than nine in the 4th quarter.

JOHN KRINGAS

JIM PRISCHING

Clyde Drexler and the Blazers thought they were going to force Game 7 – but Michael Jordan had other plans.

"Chicago is a team with a certain arrogance," said Portland's Buck Williams, "and now I see why. They feel they're the best team in the league and they came out and showed the world."

And especially the Trail Blazers, who seemed certain that they were going to take these often unpredictable NBA Finals to a seventh game.

The Blazers led by 15 in the first half, by 17 late in the third quarter and by 15 again with just 12 minutes of basketball left. It was the kind of basketball that overwhelmed the Lakers, the Suns and the Jazz in the playoffs.

For three quarters.

"Our guys just ran out of gas," said Blazers coach Rick Adelman. "In the fourth quarter, Chicago's defensive intensity picked up and we didn't handle the ball well and when the game was on the line, they took control."

Whether it was John Paxson spotting up or making a key steal, Michael Jordan breaking down the defense for his 33 points, Bill Cartwright and Horace Grant switching on defense when necessary, Scottie Pippen soaring for rebounds or moving the ball, or that cast of characters off the bench, the Bulls were just too hot for Portland to handle.

"Whenever you make it to the finals," said Blazers guard Terry Porter, "and you lose, it's disappointing. But the sun will still come up tomorrow."

And shine on another - hard to keep saying that word - Chicago NBA championship.

— Sam Smith

PARTY TIME!

Champs reward fans with postgame love-in

Bulls owner Jerry Reinsdorf, who is Chief Sitting Bull, insisted on championship night that he would take his throbbing head and plop it into the chair at 8 a.m. the next morning for a dentist's appointment, as scheduled.

But would the dentist show? Did anybody in Chicago go to work that Monday?

Game 7, scheduled for three nights later, if necessary, wasn't. Because the Bulls refused to lose Game 6. Because they're champions of the NBA – again.

And if Michael Jordan wrenched his foot while dancing on the scorer's table – trophy clutched to a jersey soaked by the victory bubbly earned by all that

perspiration – he has time to heal. This was a scene not televised nationally, only cherished locally. It had been 29 years since a Chicago team – the Bears of 1963 – clinched a title within the city limits. Or, to be exact, 29 years and 15 minutes.

NBC, the network that broadcast this incredible comeback, owned the rights to the immediate bedlam. The Bulls, down by 17 points late, very late, adjourned to the Blackhawks' locker room after closing out the Portland Trail Blazers 97-93. It is larger than the one assigned to pro basketball and unstained by

Bob Verdi
IN THE WAKE OF THE NEWS

Michael Jordan celebrates along with the Bulls fans after the championship is won.

DON BIERMAN

76

the bubbles of triumph. The Bulls said their prayers and sprayed each other and hugged, a routine that doesn't get old.

But upstairs, the 18,676 fans who shared chairman Reinsdorf's toothache for the worse part of two hours wouldn't leave. Security had hoped they would, calmly, if possible. A lot of game plans didn't pan out that Sunday night, however. The Trail Blazers pulled the all-time Dukakis, blowing a 79-64 lead with 12 minutes remaining. Like General Motors, Portland can't seem to string together four good quarters. The Bulls played suffocating defense; the Trail Blazers wound up gasping for air. Your cheapest polyester suit couldn't unravel any quicker.

It was pretty much over when Jordan canned a 15-foot jumper with 1:39 left. The Bulls led 93-89, and from either side of the Stadium emerged a stream of law enforcers with yellow shirts and blue pants. The deployment was designed to convert the court into a moat of sorts, but even they were cheering, for the ultimate show of force emanated from the Bulls themselves – frequently criticized, yet more often than not up to the occasion.

Which is why the customers refused to go away. They rocked, they rolled, they waited. And then, after NBC pulled the plug on America at 9 p.m., those Bulls

Bobby Hansen gives a victory salute during the final game of the championship journey.

JIM PRISCHING

78

A Bulls fan is dressed for the part of singing the final victory song at the Stadium after Game 6 of the Finals.

who needed no introduction emerged from below for the loudest of love-ins.

The people stood in place, before those precious seats that had sold for $1,000, and the players exhibited all the right stuff away from the ball, which wasn't necessary anymore, either. Then Jordan grabbed the gold and went to the air one more time, along broadcast row, between the benches. Soon, he was joined by his teammates, all of whom belonged.

And somewhere in that party was Reinsdorf, smiling all over that sore gum. He does have another account to which he'd really like to devote more time. The White Sox, after all, are well into their season. But the Bulls have conspired to make a lot of

Chicago table concern for the White Sox, Cubs and just about everything else.

He then told a little story of his early ownership days.

"We came in just after Michael started his first season, 1984," Reinsdorf related. "Lee Stern, who ran the Sting [the city's pro soccer team] and was part of our White Sox group, called to congratulate me. He also reminded me that soccer was outdrawing pro basketball in this city. Imagine that. And he was right. A lot of people lost a lot of money before this thing became stable.

"We're not the Bears yet. The Bears are No. 1. They're front page even when they're 8-8. But if we can remain competitive for the next few years, and I think we can, we'll be right. We'll have

some history behind us."

It wasn't supposed to be easy, and it wasn't. Last spring's playoff run of 15-2 was an aberration, but it didn't pacify certain experts. Phil Jackson, the coach, had lost his magic touch. Scottie Pippen, the second star in the galaxy, was too erratic. The edge was gone, the end was near, the repeat was a dream destined to beget nightmares. And so – yawn. Such panic the Bulls created. And then came that 12-minute clinic for the ages.

Does it really matter now that Michael Jordan played golf on an off day in Portland? After that championship night's drill, was Chief Sitting Bull ready for another? Did anybody in Chicago go to work that Monday morning? ●

79

Jordan gave encouragement from the bench as well as provided his usual remarkable feats on the court throughout the championship journey.

MICHAEL FRYER

THE GOOD OLD DAYS

This second championship was a promise kept

One championship is a souvenir. Two is an inventory.

They look identical, like polished twins, the pair of NBA trophies that now belong to the Bulls and, by extension and devotion, to Chicago itself.

And yet they are as distinctive as a Michael Jordan tomahawk jam from a Michael Jordan post-up jumper: one uncontested, one earned, but worth the same.

This second trophy ought to be just a little larger or come with distinctive dents, something to mark the effort it took to get it, a season of entitlement followed by playoffs of challenge.

This was the greatest of all seasons for any modern Chicago sports team because it was a promise kept. In a town that always gives its warriors "next year," this

Bernie Lincicome
IN THE WAKE OF THE NEWS

was the year after next year, and it came without regrets or alibis.

From the moment the fresh and flushed winners of 1991 joined in the Grant Park chant of "Re-peat! Re-peat!" failure was not going to be accepted, and neither

they, nor we, understood how much easier it is to put a boast on a T-shirt than in an almanac.

These Bulls were not the one-ring Bears of the '80s or the half-title Sox and Cubs, not the recent next-to-first Blackhawks, full of reasons and wishes.

The Bulls have raised the standard for all Chicago sports teams of what is acceptable. One is no longer enough.

These are, now and at last, the good old days.

Phil Jackson, the coach, has won as many NBA titles as his own mentor, Red Holzman, and more than his first teacher, Bill Fitch.

The child has exceeded the father figure, without compromising his soul.

Jerry Krause, the clerk in charge of not botching it up, can gloat without censure. This is his masterpiece as much as the Mona Lisa is for the guy who bought the frame.

For the several and scattered owners of the team and instinctive meddler Jerry Reinsdorf, they have hired well and kept quiet, equally difficult tasks. Their reward has been a limousine ride with genius, not to mention profit.

The NBA is a players' league, and it's the players who deserve today's applause and accept to-morrow's exaggeration. Scottie Pippen and Horace Grant, Bill Cartwright and John Paxson, B.J. Armstrong and Scott Williams. Their achievement has bound them to each other and to us forever.

Jordan, of course, always Jordan apart, for all this means and whatever it means, it is Jordan's fault.

His singular will and exceptional gifts are shared more deeply and more widely than even Jordan knows. This is more than just the town where Michael works, it is the town that feels better about itself because this is where Michael works.

It is, after all, only basketball, and yet it is more. It is the fertilizer of tolerance and good will. Everyone is a neighbor of a winner.

Championship rings will occupy 20 percent of Will Perdue's large and rarely used fingers. Jewelry belongs to the warriors, hardware to the landlords, the memories to us all.

There is in Portland at Nike Town, the retail museum and house of sneaker worship, a large photo of Jordan's wet and grateful face pressed against the Bulls' first NBA trophy, and the caption says something like, "Michael didn't want to let the trophy go."

Ain't it the truth. ●

A RALLYING CRY

You didn't have to strain to hear the predictions at Chicago's official celebration of the Bulls' second title. Among the thank-yous to fans and playful digs at teammates, the Bulls were not bashful about telling the faithful thousands who packed Grant Park just exactly what they wanted to hear.

"We will be back," promised Bill Cartwright, and the crowd cheered in approval.

"Let's go for a three-peat," shouted Scottie Pippen.

The rally was an intimate, purely joyous tribute that provided one more opportunity for the Bulls to thank their fans. They did not let the opportunity slip by.

"Without you guys' support, no way would we have done it twice," said Michael Jordan. "Without you guys' support, there's no way we're going to be able to do it for the third time."

The fans returned the Bulls' affection with high-decibel roars, and the championship trophy – the Bulls' second – glistened in brilliant sunlight. ●

EDUARDO CONTRERAS

EDUARDO CONTRERAS

A daredevil (above) tries to upstage activities at the Bulls rally in Grant Park with antics atop a lighting support pole. Coach Phil Jackson (opposite) arrives at the rally with a victorious gesture for the happy fans. Michael Jordan (left) and Scottie Pippen show off the NBA championship trophy.

JIM PRISCHING

THREE-PEAT?

Once, twice, it's never enough — a new chant has begun

To call it intoxicating would be only approaching the truth, for it is downright addictive.

Victory. Success. Adulation. One time. Twice. It is never enough.

Even for the media, both harried and drained after covering the Bulls through their second magical season, that Sunday night was irresistible.

To watch a team strive for a goal shared by 27 other teams; to witness the natural travails that befall all athletes during the course of a long season; and then to see the total effort come to fruition is, despite the professional distance, stirring to say the least.

The oldest and most frequently used sports cliché on record has to be, "We're going to take it

Can Jordan continue to mystify, to be ready to salvage victory when the task seems too much for others?

one game at a time." So when that stubborn caution finally falls as it did on June 14, 1992, the emotions are understandably boundless.

To see Michael Jordan, shirt untucked, championship cap

Melissa Isaacson

askew, cigar in one hand, game ball in the other, doing a celebratory jig on the Stadium scorers' table and beckoning his teammates to join him, was both surreal and captivating.

And to watch the greatest party the 63-year-old building had ever hosted fade later to a scene of discarded cups, stomped-out cigars and the keyboards' ever-present clattering echoing through the now-empty arena, was to understand what made John Paxson so sentimental the morning after.

"It's not real," he would say not 12 hours later. "And those moments go by so quickly, you

can't recapture them again. That's why we wanted to do it again."

And that is why the crowd's chants of "Three-peat" began scarcely seconds after the chants of "Repeat." Why, for the Bulls, this season had been one long ordeal of defending their past success while trying desperately to satisfy future expectations.

But all the time they complained about the scrutiny and resulting pressure, even they understood.

"There's only one way to achieve something once you've won," Paxson would say while the champagne still flowed, "and that's to win again. That's why this is so special."

And so it will be up to this team, to whoever occupies the red and white jerseys, to live up to 1991 and 1992. To continue living up to it.

Including the Bulls, just four NBA franchises have ever won two world championships in a row. Only two have won three or more consecutive titles.

"Three-peat."

An inspiring cry in the hours and days after that fateful Sunday night but, undoubtedly, it will become a haunting one as time goes on.

"Three-peat."

Can Jordan continue to mystify, to not merely perform at a superhuman level night after night, but be ready to salvage victory when the task seems too much for others?

Can Scottie Pippen continue to explore the boundaries of his vast potential while dealing with the inherent consequences of not succeeding quite fast enough?

Can Horace Grant's body continue to take the pounding, his will the fatigue and his pride the reality of a role which never will be considered glamorous?

Can Bill Cartwright and John Paxson continue to ignore their aching knees and sore backs, ignore the very march of time, to see the Bulls break new ground?

Can the team avoid serious injury, dissension and complacency? And can the Bulls bench continue to deal with the uncertainty of Phil Jackson's rotation while remaining prepared, as they did in the deciding game against Portland, to step in and save the day?

As Paxson said, it will be the only measure of future achievement.

Unfair or not, that is the bur-

Cliff Levingston shares the Bulls' championship trophy with the Stadium crowd.

den these Bulls carry with them as they attempt to satisfy a craving that will no doubt re-emerge.

One or more of them will flick on their VCRs and there it will be again. The postgame frenzy, the table-top dance, the pure satisfaction of a goal accomplished and the unadulterated adoration

of some 18,000 Bulls fans enveloping them.

Eventually, the camera will pan to Jordan and if they look closely, they will see his right hand displaying what looks a lot like the universal sign for OK.

But it is not, of course. It is three fingers. Sure as can be. ●

Bulls 1991-92 regular-season statistics

Player	G	GS	Avg min	FG	FG-A	Pct	3 pt	3 pt-A	FT	FT-A	Pct
Michael Jordan	80	80	38.8	943	1818	.519	27	100	491	590	.832
Scottie Pippen	82	82	38.6	687	1359	.506	16	80	330	434	.760
Horace Grant	81	81	35.3	457	790	.578	0	2	235	317	.741
B.J. Armstrong	82	3	22.9	335	697	.481	35	87	104	129	.806
Bill Cartwright	64	64	23.0	208	445	.467	0	0	96	159	.604
John Paxson	79	79	24.6	257	487	.528	12	44	29	37	.784
Stacey King	79	12	16.1	215	425	.506	2	5	119	158	.753
Will Perdue	77	7	13.1	152	278	.547	1	2	45	91	.495
Craig Hodges	56	2	9.9	93	242	.384	36	96	16	17	.941
Cliff Levingston	79	0	12.9	125	251	.498	1	6	60	96	.625
Scott Williams	63	0	11.0	83	172	.483	0	3	48	74	.649
Bobby Hansen	66	0	11.7	75	169	.444	7	25	8	22	.364
BULLS*	82	—	241.8	3643	7168	.508	138	454	1587	2132	.744
Opponents	82	—	241.8	3206	6970	.460	218	657	1525	1985	.768

Player	Off reb	Def reb	Tot reb	Ast	PF	Dq	Stls	Tot	Blks	Pts	Avg	High
Michael Jordan	91	420	511	489	201	1	182	200	75	2404	30.1	51
Scottie Pippen	185	445	630	572	242	2	155	253	93	1720	21.0	41
Horace Grant	344	463	807	217	196	0	100	98	131	1149	14.2	28
B.J. Armstrong	19	126	145	266	88	0	46	94	5	809	9.9	22
Bill Cartwright	93	231	324	87	131	0	22	75	14	512	8.0	17
John Paxson	21	75	96	241	142	0	49	44	9	555	7.0	16
Stacey King	87	118	205	77	129	0	21	76	25	551	7.0	23
Will Perdue	108	204	312	80	133	1	16	72	43	350	4.5	16
Craig Hodges	7	17	24	54	33	0	14	22	1	238	4.3	21
Cliff Levingston	109	118	227	66	134	0	27	42	45	311	3.9	13
Scott Williams	90	157	247	50	122	0	13	35	36	214	3.4	12
Bobby Hansen	15	58	73	68	128	0	26	28	3	165	2.5	13
BULLS*	1173	2439	3612	2279	1693	4	672	1088	480	9011	109.9	140
Opponents	1081	2171	3252	1841	1800	15	631	1288	352	8155	99.5	126

* Bulls totals include statistics from Mark Randall, Dennis Hopson, Rory Sparrow and Chuck Nevitt, who were released or traded early in the season.

Bulls 1992 playoff statistics

Player	G	Avg min	FG	FG-A	Pct	3 pt	3 pt-A	FT	FT-A	Pct
Michael Jordan	22	41.8	290	581	.499	17	44	162	189	.857
Scottie Pippen	22	40.9	152	325	.468	6	24	118	155	.761
Horace Grant	22	38.9	99	183	.541	0	2	51	76	.671
John Paxson	22	27.2	73	139	.525	12	27	16	19	.842
B.J. Armstrong	22	19.7	63	139	.453	5	17	30	38	.789
Bill Cartwright	22	27.8	55	116	.474	0	0	13	31	.419
Scott Williams	22	14.6	34	70	.486	0	1	20	28	.714
Stacey King	14	7.9	18	40	.450	2	2	15	23	.652
Cliff Levingston	22	8.7	25	57	.439	0	1	14	28	.500
Will Perdue	18	8.7	18	37	.486	0	1	9	20	.450
Craig Hodges	17	8.1	16	41	.390	9	20	1	2	.500
Bobby Hansen	9	7.7	9	22	.409	3	6	1	3	.333
BULLS	22	241.1	852	1750	.487	54	145	450	612	.735
Opponents	22	241.1	767	1708	.449	65	206	473	615	.769

Player	Off reb	Def reb	Tot reb	Ast	PF	Dq	Stls	Tot	Blks	Pts	Avg	High
Michael Jordan	37	100	137	127	62	0	44	81	16	759	34.5	56
Scottie Pippen	59	134	193	147	72	1	41	70	25	428	19.5	31
Horace Grant	76	118	194	66	68	1	24	21	39	249	11.3	20
John Paxson	0	22	22	61	53	1	14	13	1	174	7.9	16
B.J. Armstrong	2	22	24	47	33	0	14	18	0	161	7.3	18
Bill Cartwright	29	69	98	38	70	1	11	27	4	123	5.6	12
Scott Williams	33	62	95	7	65	0	6	15	18	88	4.0	12
Stacey King	7	13	20	5	12	0	5	10	2	53	3.8	13
Cliff Levingston	17	24	41	9	31	0	4	11	6	64	2.9	12
Will Perdue	18	22	40	9	34	1	3	12	10	45	2.5	16
Craig Hodges	3	1	4	5	10	0	5	8	0	42	2.5	7
Bobby Hansen	4	5	9	10	10	0	1	2	0	22	2.4	5
BULLS	285	592	877	531	520	5	172	298	121	2208	100.4	122
Opponents	281	584	865	502	539	10	155	328	88	2072	94.2	115

BULLS
Da Champs!

The following people contributed to the Chicago Tribune's coverage of the 1991-92 championship season of the Chicago Bulls:

SPORTS

Associate Managing Editor/Sports: Richard Leslie
Sports Editor: Bob Condor
Associate Editors: Bill Hageman, Jim Masek, Ken Paxson, Bob Vanderberg
Assistant Editors: Jim Binkley, Tom Carkeek, Joseph Knowles
Reporters: Melissa Isaacson, Sam Smith, Paul Sullivan, Skip Myslenski, Mike Conklin, Robert Markus, Steve Nidetz, Don Pierson, Ed Sherman
Columnists: Bernie Lincicome, Bob Verdi
Copy Editors: Claudia Banks, Bob Fischer, Dan Gibbard, Julie Hanna, Jim Harding, K.C. Johnson, Chris Kuc, Rich La Susa, Rebecca Morrissey, Dan Moulton, Gary Reinmuth, Mark Shapiro, Ed Stone, Rich Strom, Jack Thompson, Tim Tierney
Makeup: John Blais, Victor Chi, Mike Esposito, Mike Hanlon, Rick Maupin, Gene McCormick, Norm Unger,
Editorial Assistants: Cynthia Curry-Bennett, Tony Tranchita
Staff: Bernie Colbeck, Steve Mauzer, Rose Sukowski

PHOTOGRAPHY

Director of Photography: Phil Greer
Chief Photographer: Jose More
Picture Editor: Karen Engstrom
Assignment Editor: Don Bierman
Assistant Picture Editors: Tim Broekema, Wendy White, Randy Wood
Photographers: Charles Cherney, Eduardo Contreras, Michael Fryer, John Kringas, Val Mazzenga, Michael Meinhardt, Charles Osgood, Jose Osorio, Jim Prisching, Nancy Stone, George Thompson, Ed Wagner
Photo Lab Technicians: Jim Badali, Olavs Borg, Kathleen Celer, Prisana Kongsuwan, Anthony Simmons, Art Walker

GRAPHICS

Associate Managing Editor/Photo, Art, Graphics: George Langford
Illustrations Editor: Stephen Cvengros
Artists/Researchers: Pat Bergner, Vasin Omer D., Martin Fischer, Tracy Herman, Scott Holingue, Tom Irvine, David Jahntz, Steve Little, Dennis Odom, Stephen Ravenscraft, Nancy I. Z. Reese, Don Sena, Julie Sheer, Rick Tuma, Terry Volpp

RESEARCH

Photos: Jonas Baltrukonis, Abby DeShane, Steve Marino, Judi Marriott, Cynthia Marshall, Mary Wilson, Leida Woodham
Editorial Material: Karen Blair, Mary Huschen, Joe Pete, Alan Peters, Barbara Sherlock, Wanda Whiteside

PRE-PRESS

Color Prepress Department Manager: Bruce Wade
Color Prepress Supervisors: James P. Conner, Joe Rodriguez, Donald Wresch
Planners: Ramona Jones, Maritza Martinez, Eric Shiplock
Proofer/Plotters: Jennifer Baas, Ron Garde, Jose Trevino
Color Systems Operators: Charles Boyce, Ted Golaszewski, Tom Gruzlewski, Joseph Lamantia, Mike Luczak, James Pinzine, Terri Sticha
Color Scanner Operators: James Jurewicz, Karen Merwick, Ed Zurbano

JIM PRISCHING